Day H

UNIVERSITY PRESS OF FLORIDA

Florida A&M University, Tallahassee
Florida Atlantic University, Boca Raton
Florida Gulf Coast University, Ft. Myers
Florida International University, Miami
Florida State University, Tallahassee
New College of Florida, Sarasota
University of Central Florida, Orlando
University of Florida, Gainesville
University of North Florida, Jacksonville
University of South Florida, Tampa
University of West Florida, Pensacola

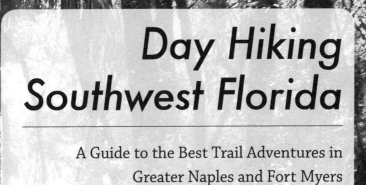

Day Hiking Southwest Florida

A Guide to the Best Trail Adventures in
Greater Naples and Fort Myers

JOHNNY MOLLOY

University Press of Florida
Gainesville · Tallahassee · Tampa · Boca Raton
Pensacola · Orlando · Miami · Jacksonville · Ft. Myers · Sarasota

VIVA FLORIDA 500
1513-2013

A Florida Quincentennial Book

All photos are by the author.

This book may be available in an electronic edition.

19 18 17 16 15 14   6 5 4 3 2 1

Library of Congress Cataloging-in-Publication Data
Molloy, Johnny, 1961– author.
Day hiking Southwest Florida : a guide to the best trail adventures in greater
Naples and Fort Myers / Johnny Molloy.
pages cm
ISBN 978-0-8130-4946-5
1. Hiking—Florida—Naples—Guidebooks. 2. Hiking—Florida—Fort Myers—
Guidebooks. 3. Trails—Florida—Naples—Guidebooks. 4. Trails—Florida—
Fort Myers—Guidebooks. 5. Naples (Fla.)—Guidebooks. 6. Fort Myers (Fla.)—
Guidebooks. I. Title.
GV199.42.F62N375 2014
796.51097594—dc23
2013038958

The University Press of Florida is the scholarly publishing agency for the State
University System of Florida, comprising Florida A&M University, Florida
Atlantic University, Florida Gulf Coast University, Florida International
University, Florida State University, New College of Florida, University of
Central Florida, University of Florida, University of North Florida, University
of South Florida, and University of West Florida.

University Press of Florida
15 Northwest 15th Street
Gainesville, FL 32611-2079
http://www.upf.com

This book is for all the trail builders and hikers
who wander the trails of Southwest Florida.

Contents

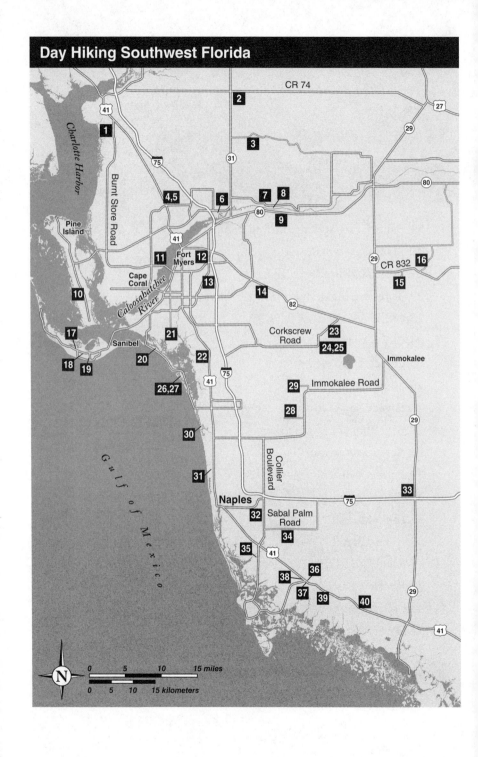

Day Hiking Southwest Florida

Hike Locator Map

1 Charlotte Harbor Preserve
2 Footprints Trail
3 Babcock Ranch Ecotour Trail
4 Prairie Pines Preserve North Loop
5 Prairie Pines Preserve South Loop
6 Caloosahatchee Creeks East Preserve
7 Telegraph Creek Preserve
8 Caloosahatchee Regional Park
9 Hickeys Creek Mitigation Park
10 Pine Island Flatwoods Preserve
11 Four Mile Cove Ecological Center
12 Calusa Nature Center
13 Six Mile Cypress Slough Preserve
14 Wild Turkey Strand Preserve
15 Tram Trail
16 Twin Mill Trail
17 Indigo Trail at Ding Darling Refuge
18 Sanibel-Captiva Nature Center
19 Bailey Tract at Ding Darling Refuge
20 Matanzas Pass Preserve
21 Estero Bay Preserve Hike

22 Koreshan State Historic Site Hike
23 CREW Marsh Hike
24 CREW Cypress Dome Hike
25 Caracara Prairie Preserve
26 Black Island Trail
27 Lovers Key Trail and Beach Walk
28 Bird Rookery Swamp Loop
29 Corkscrew Swamp Sanctuary
30 Barefoot Beach Preserve Hike
31 Clam Pass Park
32 Lasip Mitigation Park
33 Duncan Trail
34 Sabal Palm Trail
35 Rookery Bay Hike
36 Collier-Seminole Hiking Adventure Trail
37 Royal Palm Nature Trail
38 Collier-Seminole Hike/Bike Trail
39 Marsh Trail
40 Big Cypress Bend Boardwalk

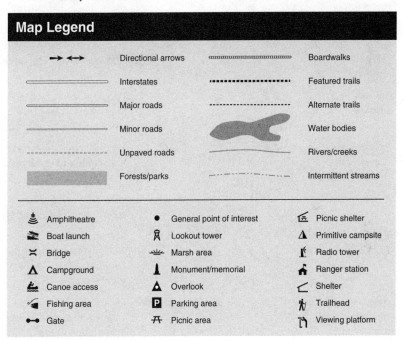

Map Legend

➡ ↔	Directional arrows	▬▬▬▬▬▬	Boardwalks
	Interstates	• • • • • • • •	Featured trails
	Major roads	- - - - - - - -	Alternate trails
	Minor roads		Water bodies
	Unpaved roads		Rivers/creeks
	Forests/parks		Intermittent streams

♨ Amphitheatre		● General point of interest		🏕 Picnic shelter	
⛵ Boat launch		🯅 Lookout tower		◭ Primitive campsite	
⋈ Bridge		⟡ Marsh area		📡 Radio tower	
⛺ Campground		▮ Monument/memorial		🏠 Ranger station	
🛶 Canoe access		◭ Overlook		⟨ Shelter	
🎣 Fishing area		🅿 Parking area		🚶 Trailhead	
•–• Gate		⊼ Picnic area		🯆 Viewing platform	

Hikes at a Glance

Hike	Distance (miles)	Time (hours)	Difficulty	Highlights
1 Charlotte Harbor Preserve	2.6	1.5	Easy	Explore coastal maritime woods
2 Footprints Trail	2.4	1.5	Easy–moderate	Wildlife viewing, swamp slogging
3 Babcock Ranch Ecotour Trail	2.3	1.5	Easy	Pair your hike through palmetto prairies with an ecotour
4 Prairie Pines Preserve North Loop	9.8	6.0	Difficult	Enjoy a long hike in a large land parcel with vegetational variety
5 Prairie Pines Preserve South Loop	8.0	5.0	Difficult	This popular circuit traverses former cattle country; see an old corral
6 Caloosahatchee Creeks East Preserve	1.4	1.0	Easy	Explore cypress swamp boardwalk and rich forests
7 Telegraph Creek Preserve	4.1	2.5	Moderate	Visit Telegraph Creek and adjacent Bob Janes Preserve
8 Caloosahatchee Regional Park	3.2	2.0	Moderate	Soak in riverside hammock while gaining vistas of the Caloosahatchee River at this excellent park
9 Hickeys Creek Mitigation Park	5.8	3.5	Moderate	Make a triple loop through varied landscape and visit lush Hickeys Creek

Hike	Distance (miles)	Time (hours)	Difficulty	Highlights
10 Pine Island Flatwoods Preserve	1.4	1.0	Easy	Loop through native pines and flats of palmetto on Pine Island
11 Four Mile Cove Ecological Preserve	1.7	1.5	Easy	Explore mangrove forests along Caloosahatchee River in Cape Coral
12 Calusa Nature Center	1.9	1.5	Easy	Combine hike with trip to aviary and museum
13 Six Mile Cypress Slough Preserve	1.2	1.0	Easy	Stroll a boardwalk through varied wetlands
14 Wild Turkey Strand Preserve	1.8	2.0	Easy	Combine hiking and history, touring restored forests and wetlands at site of WW II training station
15 Tram Trail	3.6	3.0	Moderate	Take a sun-splashed hike atop an old logging tram road at Okaloacoochee Slough State Forest
16 Twin Mill Trail	2.4	2.0	Moderate	Enjoy solitude aplenty on this historic loop at Okaloacoochee Slough State Forest.
17 Indigo Trail at Ding Darling Refuge	4.1	2.5	Moderate	Enjoy a trek on this Sanibel Island national wildlife preserve
18 Sanibel-Captiva Nature Center	1.9	1.5	Easy	This hike explores the interior of Sanibel Island and features views from an observation tower
19 Bailey Tract at Ding Darling Refuge	1.4	1.0	Easy	This loop, a favorite of bird-watchers, visits freshwater ponds and is popular with locals for daily exercise
20 Matanzas Pass Preserve	1.4	1.5	Easy	Hike one of the last remaining native plant communities on Estero Island.

(continued)

Hike	Distance (miles)	Time (hours)	Difficulty	Highlights
21 Estero Bay Preserve Hike	2.5	1.5	Moderate	Barren salt flats, tidal marsh, and mangrove patches fashion a unique hiking palette to explore.
22 Koreshan State Historic Site Hike	1.8	3.5	Easy	Explore a fascinating historic locale, the preserved site of the Koreshan Unity Settlement.
23 CREW Marsh Hike	3.0	2.0	Moderate	Visit a host of Southwest Florida environments before soaking in panoramic views from an observation tower.
24 CREW Cypress Dome Hike	4.4	2.5	Moderate	Experience solitude in protected wildland, highlighted by a tropical hardwood hammock.
25 Caracara Prairie Preserve	5.0	3.0	Moderate	Enjoy palms and prairies in this tract named for an uncommon Florida raptor.
26 Black Island Trail	2.6	1.5	Easy	Hike beside mangrove-lined waterways on groomed pathway at picturesque Lovers Key State Park
27 Lovers Key Trail and Beach Walk	4.5	3.0	Moderate	Combine two scenic ecosystems—maritime forests and Gulf Coast beaches—on one hike.
28 Bird Rookery Swamp Loop	12.0	7.0	Difficult	This long hike traverses some of the most remote terrain in Southwest Florida
29 Corkscrew Swamp Sanctuary	2.2	3.0	Easy	Stroll a two-plus-mile boardwalk through the last remaining old-growth cypress swamp forest in the area.

Hike	Distance (miles)	Time (hours)	Difficulty	Highlights
30 Barefoot Beach Preserve Hike	3.0	2.0	Moderate	Hike through the island interior and along the beach at this barrier-island preserve.
31 Clam Pass Park	1.2	1.0	Easy	Elevated boardwalk leads through mangroves to the beach.
32 Lasip Mitigation Park	1.1	1.0	Easy	Loop your way through restored forestland in a busy part of Collier County.
33 Duncan Trail	1.4	1.0	Easy	Visit diverse habitats at important panther refuge.
34 Sabal Palm Trail	3.5	2.0	Moderate	Travel the back of beyond at Picayune State Forest.
35 Rookery Bay Hike	1.4	1.5	Easy	Visit impressive visitor center before walking woods with old pioneer homesite.
36 Collier-Seminole Hiking Adventure Trail	7.4	4.5	Difficult	This challenging trail loops through secluded terrain at Collier-Seminole State Park.
37 Royal Palm Nature Trail	0.9	1.0	Easy	This nature trail traverses a tropical hardwood forest as well as an extensive boardwalk.
38 Collier-Seminole Hike/ Bike Trail	3.5	2.0	Moderate	Take a walk on the historic side as you trace the old San Marco Road.
39 Marsh Trail	2.4	2.0	Easy	Path leads to a wildlife observation tower with a commanding view, ideal for seeing birdlife below.
40 Big Cypress Bend Boardwalk	1.2	1.0	Easy	Walk beneath huge cypresses and strangler figs in a riot of vegetational variety.

Preface and Acknowledgments

When thinking of Florida, I recall its vast natural resources, from the Tallahassee Hills to the lakes of the central state, the beaches of the Everglades, and the islands of the Keys. Others may see the state through a different lens, but I love Florida's great outdoors and the opportunities that it presents. Southwest Florida, despite heavy growth pressure, harbors abundant outdoor attractions—including hiking—for those looking to get back to nature on nature's terms. I hope this guide leads you on as many enjoyable adventures as I have had in Southwest Florida, from the trails of Charlotte Harbor Preserve up near Punta Gorda to the backcountry of Collier-Seminole State Park down Everglades City way.

Hiking the trails of this area has been a great joy and an engaging experience. I have encountered abundant natural splendor while working on this book. Certain scenes immediately come to mind—sunlight piercing the magnificent pine stands at Picayune State Forest, or shorebirds dancing on the sandy beaches at Lovers Key State Park. I recall walking through the strange salt flats of Estero Bay Preserve, or atop the boardwalk at brooding Corkscrew Swamp Sanctuary, where five-hundred-year-old cypresses rise from the depths. I hear Hickeys Creek noisily flow among queer cypress knees. I feel chill morning air while gazing on the flats of Prairie Pines Preserve. I sense the density of vegetation while traversing a hardwood hammock at Okaloacoochee Slough State Forest. I smell the tidal waters rising near a boardwalk at Matanzas Pass Preserve. I feel the hot sun while hiking across open palmetto prairie at Pine Island Flatwoods Preserve.

I recall a wealth of superlative scenery that can be found along the hiking trails of these Southwest Florida treasures.

And what a treat it was to absorb the best scenes along the best hikes that together paint a mosaic of ecosystems within park and preserve lands stretching across Greater Fort Myers and Naples! I took the duty very seriously, drawing upon my years of experience exploring the Sunshine State and authoring more than fifty outdoor guides, including several specific to Florida. I wanted to get it right. To this end, I included hikes that paint an accurate picture of what Southwest Florida has to offer. May you find the hikes presented here as rewarding as I have.

Throughout the process, I kept looking for the best of the best and found some new sights—panoramas of the Caloosahatchee River from Four Mile Cove Ecological Center, the birder's paradise of the Marsh Trail at Ten Thousand Islands National Wildlife Refuge, and fascinating maritime woods at Sanibel-Captiva Nature Center. After writing this book, I came away with an even more profound respect for the preserved parcels of Southwest Florida. I hope you will, too. Happy hiking!

Thanks to the University Press of Florida, especially Meredith Morris-Babb, and to all the people who have hiked with me in the Sunshine State.

Introduction

At first thought, Fort Myers and Naples may not seem like hiker towns—nor may Southwest Florida in general. Read on, however, and you just may change your mind. The land—and water—of Southwest Florida was originally part of the great sheet flow of the Everglades, where the lakes of Central Florida flowed south down the Kissimmee River into great Lake Okeechobee, which, during the rainy season, in turn overflowed down the Caloosahatchee River through what is now Fort Myers and into the Gulf. Other strands imperceptibly moved south and west, along creeks and streams and the famous inches-deep sheet flow through the sawgrass. In other, higher places, a host of ecosystems rose, the vast pine flatwoods stretching to the horizon, deep tropical hammocks—Florida's jungles—where live oak, gumbo-limbo, and strangler fig grew in inconceivable profusion. In still other spots, palms rose together by the thousands, forming green-fronded cathedrals above an open floor. Closer to the salt water, mangrove-lined, winding waterways merged into tidal streams, quiet coves, and open bays. As the sheet flow reached the Gulf, it met mainland beaches and barrier islands dotting the saline waters, always subject to the landscape-altering hurricanes.

This was the land ruled by the Calusa, who mercilessly lorded over Southwest Florida, then lost their homeland to more powerful Europeans. The United States was born, but Southwest Florida remained a sleepy backwater, a place where fishermen resided on the coast and the cracker cowboys tamed the interior.

Then came loggers, dredges, land booms, and air-conditioning, in that order. Southwest Florida began to change and grow, yet remained the little brother of what became the metropolis on Florida's east coast, inching from Miami to Martin County.

Southwest Florida saw how the other side grew and evolved, and learned from Miami's mistakes. It also had the advantage of growing in a later, more environmentally aware era, in which conservation of land and water has proven itself to be both ecologically and economically smart. Lands have been acquired publicly and privately for their intrinsic natural and scenic value, and also to protect, manage, and maintain the above-ground flow of water and the underground aquifer from which Southwest Florida obtains its drinking water.

So how does all this make Fort Myers and Naples hiker towns? An array of trails have been built in the preserved lands of Southwest Florida. The Corkscrew Regional Ecosystem Watershed (CREW) lands offer a good example. Part of Corkscrew Swamp, comprising 60,000 acres in Lee and Collier Counties, these lands have been purchased and set aside. During the wet season, the CREW lands soak in precipitation, filtering the water before it descends into the porous rock strata below the land's surface that hold much of Southwest Florida's drinking water. Recharge zones such as the CREW lands not only protect Southwest Florida's water supply but also provide hiking trails for the public's recreational use and habitat for the local flora and fauna.

Also, simply seeing the natural treasures lost in fast-growing Florida has stimulated citizens to act now to conserve some lands. Lee County's Conservation 20/20 program purchases lands of environmental significance and provides public recreation opportunities. Conservation Collier is a similar county program designed to preserve rare habitats and create public greenspace. Trails have been built in many of the county preserves, providing us with additional walking opportunities.

Private organizations have stepped in, too, conserving lands and creating trails that allow us to view these parcels. Corkscrew Swamp Sanctuary is a good example, as is Calusa Nature Center. Additionally, the State of Florida has established several state parks in Southwest Florida. Collier-Seminole, Lovers Key State Park, and Cayo Costa State Park each features pathways traversing a montage of landscapes. Other state lands such as Picayune State Forest add still more trail destinations. Then mix in federal properties, such as Ten Thousand Islands and Florida Panther National Wildlife Refuges, and you have significant and varied destinations with miles and miles of trails. Southwest Florida truly is a hiker's paradise.

The Calusa knew Southwest Florida as a special spot whose incredible biodiversity radiated God's glory. Today, it is where Fort Myers and Naples form twin pulses of growing cities, modern hiker towns. The creation of parks and preserves and building trails within benefits us twenty-first-century residents. I hope the hikes offered in this book help you explore, understand, and appreciate the natural and human history of the special slice of the Sunshine State. Enjoy.

How to Use This Guide

Each hike has its own unique description. A short hike summary is located at the beginning of each hike. It gives an overview of what the hike is like—the terrain, what you might see along the way, and why you should go. Following the hike summary is an information box that allows the hiker quick access to pertinent information: hike distance, time, difficulty, highlights, cautions, fees/permits, best seasons, other trail users, and trail contacts. An example of a box included with a hike is given below:

CREW Marsh Hike

Hike Summary: This hike explores a host of Southwest Florida environments—pine flatwoods, seasonal marshes, tropical hardwood hammocks, and wooded sloughs in a large, wildlife-rich habitat. Your loop, on well-marked paths, leads to an observation deck alongside a seasonal pond before coming to a high tower overlooking the large wildland. Soak in panoramic views before crossing a dark cypress slough. The rich forest continues as you enter a live oak hammock. Reemerge into pines, completing the circuit.

Distance: 3.0-mile loop
Hiking Time: 2.0 hours
Difficulty: Moderate
Highlights: Multiple ecosystems, observation tower
Cautions: None
Fees/Permits: No fees or permits required
Best Seasons: November through April
Other Trail Users: None. Leashed dogs allowed.
Trail Contacts: CREW Land & Water Trust, 23998 Corkscrew Road, Estero, FL 33928, (239) 657-2253, www.crewtrust.org
Finding the Trailhead: From exit 123 on I-75, travel 22 miles east on Corkscrew Rd. You will pass the CREW Cypress Dome Trails 3.4 miles before reaching the CREW Marsh trails, on your right.
GPS Trailhead Coordinates: N26° 29.510', W81° 32.031'

From the information box, we can learn the details of each particular hike. This hike is 3.0 miles long and forms a loop. "Hiking Time" is the average time it will take to cover the route. "Hiking Time" factors in total distance and trail conditions. Factor your own fitness level into the given hiking time. "Highlights" describes the can't-miss part of the trek. "Cautions" reviews any potential hiking hazards, so you can be aware on the front end. Obviously, this does not cover every potential pitfall of a given hike, but it does keep you apprised of any hike-specific hazards. "Fees/Permits" lets you know ahead of time if there is a charge to park or enter a particular place, or whether a permit is required to hike or camp. "Best Seasons" lists the time of year when this hike is most rewarding. "Other Trail Users" informs as to whether the path is hiker-only or also shared with bicyclers or equestrians. It also notes whether dogs are allowed on the hike. "Trail Contacts" details ways to reach the particular governing body of the given hike, including mailing address, phone number, and website. "Finding the Trailhead" gives specific directions from a commonly known given location to the hike's starting point, most often the nearest interstate. "GPS Trailhead Coordinates" enables you to use your navigational aid to find the trailhead as well.

Following each box is a narrative describing the hike. In this detailed account, trail junctions, stream bridges, overlooks, and trailside features are noted along with their distance from the trailhead. This helps keep you apprised of your whereabouts and helps to make sure you don't miss any noted features. A summary of trail mileage is given at the narrative's end, so you can quickly scan the distance to major trail intersections or highlights. All the above information should help you make the most of these Southwest Florida hikes. Now get out there and hit the trail!

Weather

The climate of Southwest Florida attracts a lot of residents and winter visitors. Winter and the dry season bring warm, clear days and mild nights, though cold fronts punch down occasionally, bringing chilly temperatures. Even then, daytime highs usually reach shirtsleeve level. Rain occasionally comes with the fronts, and storms sometimes drift in from the Gulf. Summer warm-up begins in April, and people start thinking about the three h's—heat, haze, and humidity. Afternoon thunderstorms are common, with tropical storms and hurricanes a threat until November. The Gulf region does not receive as strong or frequent breezes as on the Atlantic side, resulting in some sweltering summer days.

For most trail trekkers, the hiking season starts when the first cool winds push into the Gulf Coast in late October. Hikers are found regularly on the trails until the rainy season begins in June. However, early-morning hikers can be found on the trails throughout the year.

The chart below details the average monthly temperatures for Fort Myers, along with precipitation.

Month	Aver. High	Aver. Low	Precipitation
January	75 degrees	54 degrees	1.9 inches
February	77	56	2.2
March	80	59	2.8
April	85	63	2.2
May	89	69	2.7
June	92	74	10.1
July	92	75	9.0
August	92	75	10.1
September	91	74	8.3
October	87	69	2.9
November	81	62	2.0
December	77	56	1.7

Hiking Considerations for Southwest Florida Day Hikers

Clothing/Footwear

Hiking in Southwest Florida requires more clothing for reasons you might not expect. Major concerns are rain, sun, insects, and cold. Yes, cold happens in Southwest Florida. When the north winds blow, add clothing in layers—a light wool sweater and/or some type of synthetic apparel in addition to the layer next to your skin. This allows you to adjust your clothing with the changes in temperature. For rain, carry a poncho at minimum. A poncho can be a good choice, as it is not as stifling as a full-blown rain jacket or rain suit, inside which heat will build.

Sun is a major consideration here. Many hiking areas are open overhead, and Sol can beat down and burn the unprepared. A shade-producing hat, long-sleeved shirt, and long pants will keep potentially damaging sun off you. A neckerchief and sunscreen will further protect you. The very same clothing that screens you from Sol will also keep the bugs at bay, for clothes are the best protection against the swamp angels, no-see-ums, and other little pests.

Footwear is another concern. Though sandals or tennis shoes may seem like the logical choice, many Southwest Florida trails are muddy and uneven. Tennis shoes may not offer enough support. Sport sandals leave much of your foot exposed. Mosquito-bitten ankles or a sliced foot far from the trailhead will make for a miserable limp back to the car. Boots and light hiking shoes are the footwear of choice. I prefer lightweight hiking boots with a minimum of leather, so the boots can dry more quickly. Strong-ankled hikers can use low-top boots.

Safety

To some outdoor enthusiasts, the forests and swamps of Southwest Florida seem laden with hazards—snakes, bears, panthers, and alligators. It is the fear of the unknown that causes this anxiety. No doubt, potentially dangerous situations can also occur in the outdoors where you live, but as long as you use sound judgment and prepare yourself before you hit the trail, you'll be much safer in the woods than most urban areas of the country. It is better to look at a hike as a fascinating discovery of the unknown rather than to become preoccupied with its potential for disaster. Here are a few tips to make your trip safer and easier:

Always bring food and water. Food will give you energy and help keep you warm, and it may sustain you in an emergency until help arrives. And you never know if there will be a stream or swamp nearby when you're thirsty. Treat your water before drinking from a stream. The chance of getting sick from the organism known as giardia or other waterborne organism is small, but there is no reason to take a chance. Boil or filter all water before drinking it. Be prepared for mosquitoes, with clothing and bug dope.

Stay on designated trails. Most hikers get lost when they leave the path. If you become disoriented, do not panic—that may result in a bad decision that will make your predicament worse. The flatwoods and wetlands of Southwest Florida offer very few high points from which to orient yourself. Retrace your steps if you can remember them, or stay put. Rangers check the trails first when searching for lost or overdue hikers.

Bring a map, a lighter, and a GPS or GPS-enabled smart phone. Should you become lost, these items can help you stick around long enough to be found or get yourself out of a pickle. Trail maps are available at ranger stations or visitor centers. Be aware of the symptoms of hypothermia—even in Florida. Shivering and forgetfulness are the two most common indicators of this cold-weather killer. Hypothermia can occur when the temperature is in the fifties, especially when a wet hiker is wearing lightweight, cotton clothing. If symptoms arise, get the victim shelter, hot liquids, and dry clothes or a dry sleeping bag.

Always bring rain gear. Thunderstorms can come on suddenly in the summer, and winter fronts can soak you to the bone. Keep in mind that a rainy day is as much a part of nature as those idyllic ones you desire. Rainy days really cut down on the crowds. With appropriate rain gear, a normally crowded trail can be a place of solitude. Do remember that getting wet opens the door to hypothermia.

Take along your brain. A cool, calculating mind is the single-most important piece of equipment you'll ever need on the trail. Think before you act. Watch your step. Plan ahead. Avoiding accidents before they happen is the best recipe for a rewarding, stress-relieving hike. Use your head out there and treat the place as if it were your own backyard.

Before you head to your chosen destination, order a map or information kit and visit the location's website. This information will help orient you to the roads, features, and attractions of your chosen hike.

Take your time along the trails. Pace yourself. Southwest Florida's wildlands are filled with wonders both big and small. We cannot always schedule our free time when we want, but try to hike during the week and to avoid the traditional holidays if possible. If you are hiking on busy days, going early in the morning will enhance your chances of seeing wildlife.

1

Charlotte Harbor Preserve

Hike Summary: This preserve presents a double-loop hike in coastal maritime woods, mangrove, along with freshwater and brackish wetlands that you cross over several bridges. This melding of ecosystems creates a rich habitat through which to hike; learn about it, too, at the park's environmental center.

The interplay of salt- and freshwater creates coastal marsh.

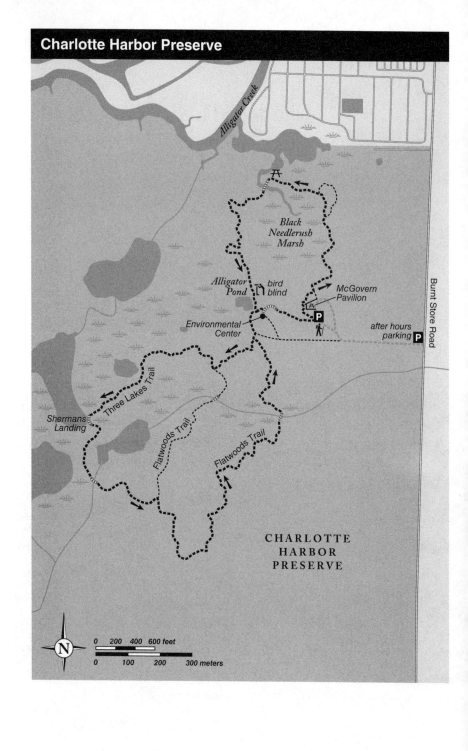

Charlotte Harbor Preserve

Alligator Creek

Black Needlerush Marsh

Alligator Pond

bird blind

McGovern Pavilion

Environmental Center

after hours parking

Burnt Store Road

Three Lakes Trail

Shermans Landing

Flatwoods Trail

Flatwoods Trail

CHARLOTTE HARBOR PRESERVE

| 0 | 200 | 400 | 600 feet |
| 0 | 100 | 200 | 300 meters |

N

Distance: 2.6-mile loop

Hiking Time: 1.5–2.5 hours

Difficulty: Easy

Highlights: Coastal maritime hammock, coastal marsh, lakes

Cautions: None

Fees/Permits: No fees or permits required

Best Seasons: November through April

Other Trail Users: None. No dogs allowed.

Trail Contacts: Charlotte Harbor Environmental Center, 10941 Burnt Store Road, Punta Gorda, FL 33955, (941) 575-5435, www.checflorida.org

Finding the Trailhead: From exit 161 on I-75 north of Fort Myers, take Charlotte County Road 768, Jones Loop Road, west for 1.5 miles to US 41. Keep straight here, as Jones Loop Road turns into Burnt Store Road. Continue for 1.2 miles more; then turn right into Charlotte Harbor Environmental Center.

GPS Trailhead Coordinates: N26° 52.453', W82° 1.628'

Back in the early 1980s, Charles E. Caniff was the catalyst behind establishing Charlotte Harbor Environmental Center, located on state property, and part of Charlotte Harbor Preserve State Park. It took him four years to get the Environmental Center up and running, working hand in hand with public officials. It was through the Environmental Center that Caniff and company began providing "environmental education, recreation, environmental research, and conservation lands management" for southwest Floridians. The Environmental Center's building is deservedly named for him. The center offers school programs, guided hikes, and other events, most of which are conducted by volunteers. Consider becoming a member of the Charlotte Harbor Environmental Center yourself. Annual dues help keep the operation going, along with donations from private companies and sponsors.

Take note: The parking area by the Environmental Center, where the trails start, is behind a gate with limited open hours. If you are there either early in the morning or late in the afternoon, park in the small parking area outside the gates by Burnt Store Road, then walk the 100 or so yards to the trailhead. To avoid parking snafus, I suggest checking the CHEC website for current hours before you come. Pass several small buildings on your way in. Near the boardwalk to the Environmental Center look right for the Eagle Point Trail and join a natural-surface path leaving right.

The natural-surface path passes the McGovern Pavilion and then tunnels beneath palms and live oaks. Cross a little boardwalk, passing a spur to the parking loop. Enter an area of pine, wax myrtle, along with scrub oak. At .3 mile, a spur trail makes a short loop and returns to the main track. Just ahead, reach Black Needlerush Marsh. This is a salt-tolerant element of the coastal marsh. At .4 mile, pass a shaded picnic area overlooking Alligator Creek. The trail then curves south over a mangrove-lined tidal stream.

At .8 mile, visit a bird blind, where you may see feeding pelicans, cormorants, or anhingas. Ahead, come to the Environmental Center and Alligator Pond. A walkway extends over the freshwater pond. It is amazing how the trail just keeps going from fresh to salt environments and back again. In places the two are commingling, of course, subject to the rise and fall of the tides.

From here, look for the sign indicating "Three Lakes Trail" and "Flatwoods Trail." Follow the two paths as they leave together from the Environmental Center in scrub oaks, palmetto, pine, and palm. At 1.0 mile, the Three Lakes Trail splits right. Take it. Explore coastal hardwood hammocks and estuarine ponds. The land is low and sometimes wet. Boardwalks help keep your feet dry in this ferny acreage. Pass Shermans Landing at 1.3 miles. Open to wide aquatic views here. This is a popular wading-bird locale. Beyond the bridge, tunnel beneath mangrove trees back into coastal marsh. The scenery keeps morphing as you traverse more boardwalks and bridges.

At 1.7 miles, meet the Flatwoods Trail. Turn right here, rejoining piney places with scattered palm hammocks, even a cedar or two. This is the land of the woodpecker and hawk. The variety of birdlife here reflects the multiplicity of environments at Alligator Creek. More bridges lie ahead, as just a nearly imperceptible elevation difference completely alters the landscape and the flora and fauna that live there. At 2.5 miles, return to the Environmental Center area. If the center is open, climb the stairs and soak in the informative offerings. Return to the trailhead by taking the boardwalk leaving the Environmental Center. It drops to ground level before reaching the trailhead at 2.6 miles.

Consider visiting Cedar Point Environmental Park, the sister preserve to this one. Charlotte County purchased the property back in 1992. Today the park presents trails and a visitor center. The series of shorter nature paths together add up to 2.6 miles of hiking possibilities in the lands astride Lemon Bay, Oyster Creek, and County Road 775. It is known for nesting bald eagles.

Mileages at a Glance

0.0 Charlotte Harbor Environmental Center trailhead

0.3 Reach Needlerush Marsh

0.9 Environmental Center

1.3 Shermans Landing

2.5 Environmental Center

2.6 Return to trailhead

2

Footprints Trail

Hike Summary: This hike traverses a montage of Southwest Florida landscapes dotting the north end of vast Babcock Ranch. Start your trek on a wide road but quickly join a singletrack blazed trail. Here, you will walk among regal live oaks, towering pines, and lower scrubby areas. Pass through an open sawgrass prairie then enter a wet cypress strand, sure to wet your feet. Turn back toward the trail, slicing through one more wet cypress strand. Discreet hikers will see not only birds, but also hogs, deer, and perhaps even a black bear.

A trail worker tests part of the pathway through a cypress stand.

Distance: 2.4-mile loop

Hiking Time: 1.5–2.0 hours

Difficulty: Easy-moderate

Highlights: Wildlife viewing, mixed woodlands, swamp slogging

Cautions: Wet cypress strands

Fees/Permits: No fees or permits required

Best Seasons: November through April

Other Trail Users: None. No dogs allowed.

Trail Contacts: Babcock Wilderness Adventures, 8000 State Road 31, Punta Gorda, FL 33982, (800) 500-5583, www.babcockwilderness .com

Finding the Trailhead: From exit 143 on I-75 northeast of Fort Myers, take Lee County 78 east 3.3 miles to FL 31 and a traffic light near the Lee County Civic Center. Turn left and take FL 31 north for 15.4 miles to Charlotte County Road 74. Turn right on Charlotte County Road 74 and travel east .4 mile. Turn into the Florida State Forest Station on your right, then right again into the designated Footprints Trail parking area.

GPS Trailhead Coordinates: N26° 56.727', W81° 45.269'

The Footprints Trail here at Babcock Ranch once consisted of two interconnected large loops that traced grassy doubletrack roads through the ranch's most northerly lands. The hike was rewarding, but arguably it was road walking. Luckily for us, some local volunteers took the trail off the roads and created a dedicated singletrack foot trail exploring the same scenic lands. The mileage went down, but after your hike here, you'll probably conclude that the quality of the Footprints Trail experience has been enhanced.

Leave the hiker trail parking area and pass around a walk-through cattle stile. Trace a raised doubletrack path south. This was originally part of the Footprints Trail. A spur road soon leaves left. Stay straight just a short distance; then at .1 mile, look left for a short boardwalk spanning a shallow canal running alongside the doubletrack grassy road. Here begins the hiker

Footprints Trail

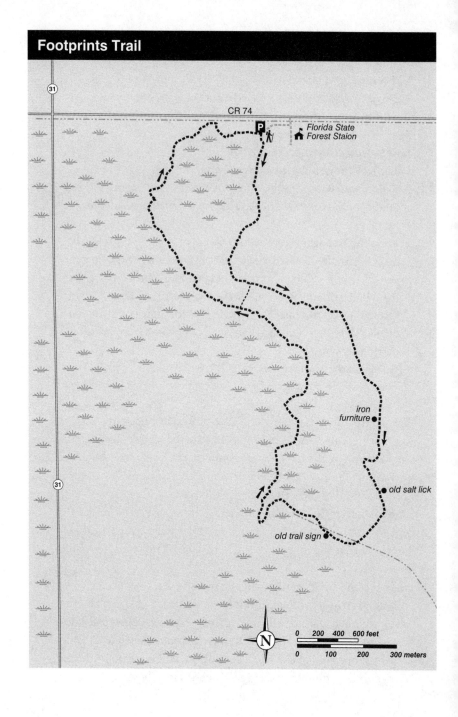

CR 74

Florida State
Forest Staion

iron
furniture

old salt lick

old trail sign

0   200   400   600 feet
0   100   200   300 meters

N

trail. If you miss the left turn, a network of grassy roads lies ahead.

The Footprints Trail is blazed in orange. Continue wandering south, winding through a live oak/palm/slash pine forest. Keep eyes and ears peeled for wildlife. I have seen deer here, and you will probably at least see sign of wild boars. At .3 mile, a short spur leads right to a grassy doubletrack, then continues to the other side of this loop, allowing for a shorter walk.

The main loop stays in a line of thick woods. An open, grassy swale extends to your right, and your woodland viewing vantage creates more wildlife observation opportunities and dramatic landscape sweeps. Cross a grassy doubletrack road at .5 mile. Keep south, still on singletrack path. At .7 mile, the trail strangely comes upon a set of iron lawn furniture, tables, chairs, and even loungers, an impromptu picnic area, nicely arranged under the outstretched arms of a live oak tree.

The Footprints Trail keeps south in mixed woods and then, at .9 mile, comes to an old wooden salt lick. Cowboys once placed salt blocks in these troughs, covered by a small tin roof, so cattle could get their nutrients.

At 1.1 miles, open onto a prairie, meeting with the now-overgrown roadbeds of the old Footprints Trail. Here, you may see a metal sign from the former route. The current Footprints Trail heads northwesterly, crisscrossing an old and shallow drainage ditch, among scattered cypresses. You have entered lower, wetter terrain. Here, the Footprints Trail lives up to its name. Look in muddy places for hog tracks, as well as oval-shaped depressions where the pigs wallow to cool down and coat themselves with mud to cut down on insect bites.

Turn north, heading through cypress strands with numerous trailside knees. Watch for these low-lying ground stumps, which will trip a hiker in no time, especially one who may be preoccupied with slopping ankle-deep in water at a few spots. Pass through a wet-for-certain area at 1.5 miles. These wetlands are rich with irises and lilies in spring.

At 1.8 miles, as you navigate a wooded strand bordered by grass and wiregrass prairie on both sides, come to a spur leading right. This is the loop shortcut. Keep straight in the palm/cypress/laurel-oak strand, slaloming among hundreds of cypress knees. An imaginative eye will see the cypress knees as spires, castles, and other structures. And those who do not see the knees at all will trip.

At 2.1 miles, watch as the blazed hiking trail cuts across some old roads. At 2.3 miles, enter a final cypress strand and turn east. Here, you enter some of the wettest and most scenic parts of the hike. Shortly emerge onto open terrain. The parking area is just ahead; you have completed the circuit.

Mileages at a Glance

0.0 Footprints Trail trailhead
0.1 Left on boardwalk, join singletrack path
0.3 Loop shortcut leaves right
0.5 Cross doubletrack
0.7 Pass iron lawn furniture
1.1 Old metal trail sign
1.8 Other end of loop shortcut
2.4 Return to trailhead

3

Babcock Ranch Ecotour Trail

Hike Summary: Southwest Florida's iconic Babcock Ranch, now a huge state wildlife management area, offers a hiking trail to complement their guided wildlife tour. Even if you want to hike only, come here to walk through Old Florida, a land of wide open spaces and lonely pine/palmetto lands. Leave the tour parking area and wander brushy woodland where you might see wild boar. Open onto pine flatwoods. Explore these secluded lands before passing by seasonal wetland, where birdlife can be found in season.

Exotic wild pigs roam through Babcock Ranch.

Distance: 2.3-mile loop
Hiking Time: 1.5–2.0 hours
Difficulty: Easy
Highlights: Palmetto prairies, wildlife viewing, ecotour
Cautions: None
Fees/Permits: No fees or permits required for hike; fee required for wildlife tour
Best Seasons: November through April
Other Trail Users: None. No dogs allowed.
Trail Contacts: Babcock Wilderness Adventures, 8000 State Road 31, Punta Gorda, FL 33982, (800) 500-5583, www.babcockwilderness .com
Finding the Trailhead: From exit 143 on I-75 northeast of Fort Myers, take Lee County 78 east 3.3 miles to FL 31 and a traffic light near the Lee County Civic Center. Turn left and take FL 31 north for 9.3 miles to the Babcock Ranch. Turn right into the ranch and follow it east for 2.3 miles to the Ecotour parking area on your right. Look for the sign indicating "Hiking Trail Parking."
GPS Trailhead Coordinates: N26° 51.397', W81° 43.253'

Babcock Ranch is a historic landmark of Southwest Florida. Over the decades, the large working ranch has been home to cattle running, vegetable growing, and fruit tree and sod farming. Coming in at more than 70,000 acres, the ranch is also home to the real Florida, left in its pristine state, a place where panthers and bears roam, where birds nest and reproduce. It also harbors part of Telegraph Swamp, an important freshwater aquifer recharge area for Southwest Florida. The public acquisition of Babcock Ranch, which stretches across Lee and Charlotte Counties, completed a corridor of wildlands connecting the Gulf of Mexico to Lake Okeechobee. This allows migration of animals, birds, and plants across this wetland ecosystem connecting the freshwater interior and the saline coast. The Babcock Ranch is managed by the Florida Division of Forestry and is thus a multiuse destination, the most popular of which are the ecotours that lead visitors throughout the ranch's natural bounty.

Babcock Ranch Ecotour Trail

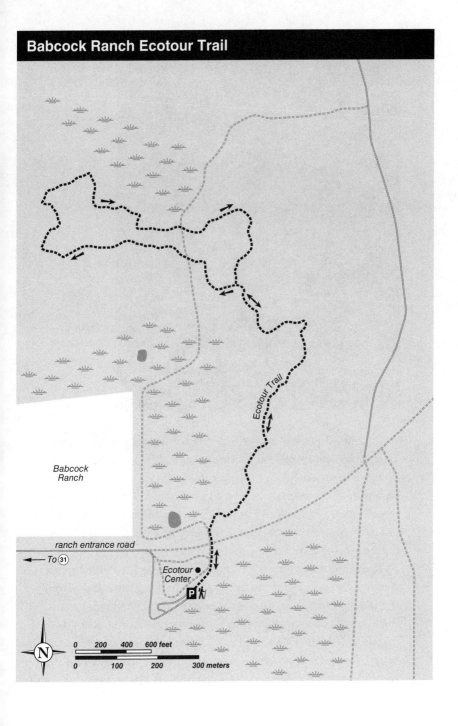

Babcock
Ranch

ranch entrance road

← To (31)

Ecotour Trail

Ecotour
Center

P ⇞

| 0 | 200 | 400 | 600 feet |
| 0 | 100 | 200 | 300 meters |

N

Seemingly humorous sign reminds hikers not to chase cows among other things.

Guided 90-minute buggy tours, by reservation only, explore Telegraph Swamp and the working parts of Babcock Ranch. Expect to see an array of critters, from alligators and birds in the swamp to farm animals on the ranch. You'll learn about Southwest Florida's human and natural history. The ranch also offers food and specialty tours. Check their website for the latest information and rates.

The Ecotour Trail begins at the same place as the guided ranch tours. Signs point you north from the parking area and across the ranch road you drove in on. Look for a trailhead kiosk marking the trail's beginning. Join a grassy track bordered by wax myrtle and head-high wiregrass. Scattered pines rise above the brush. At your feet you will undoubtedly see evidence of wild-pig rooting, and you may even see some pigs, as I have when hiking here.

At .6 mile, come to metal fences. Pass through a pair of wooden stiles, designed to keep cows from escaping but allowing hikers to pass through. The hike then enters more open terrain, heavy with low-slung palmetto. Its berries were eaten by aboriginal Floridians and are still favored by wildlife. Ahead, the mown path is signed at strategic areas to prevent your becoming lost. Signs will also warn you that the cows you may see are not tame. It is in this open area where cypress domes, pinelands, and other components of the natural Southwest Florida stretch across the distance, over which rises interposed puffy clouds and azure skies. You may hear the piercing call of a hawk in the yon.

Babcock Ranch was established by Pennsylvanian E. V. Babcock. His first Florida venture was a successful timbering company in 1889. His land holdings expanded to more than 150,000 acres. In the 1940s, E. V. Babcock's son Fred deeded more than 65,000 acres to the State of Florida. After the land was logged, it became fertile grazing and farmland. The other acreage of the original holding forms the heart of the Crescent B. Ranch, a working agricultural operation covering 153 square miles in Charlotte and Lee Counties. Crescent B. Ranch contains a wealth of native Florida ecosystems within its bounds, namely the heart of Telegraph Swamp.

At .7 mile, reach the loop portion of the hike. Stay left. Watch your footing in the uneven surface of the palmetto prairie. At 1.2 miles, come near a stretch of palms and a wetland. You will travel easterly along this seasonal swale. Ahead, a cleared trail leads left toward the pond, where bird life will be gathered in season. Turn away from the wetland back into piney woods. At 1.6 miles, complete the loop portion of the hike. From here, backtrack .6 mile to the trailhead.

Mileages at a Glance

0.0 Ecotour Trail trailhead
0.6 Begin loop portion of hike, heading left
1.2 Come near a wetland
1.6 Complete the loop portion of hike
2.3 Return to trailhead

4

Prairie Pines Preserve North Loop

Hike Summary: Enjoy a long hike in this large preserve near North Fort Myers. Walk east through pine flatwoods on a slender parcel; then reach the main wildland. Here, head north, exploring prairies, pinelands, and a hardwood hammock. This aquifer recharge area is being transformed back to native Florida vegetation from what once was melaleuca hell. After visiting the northern end of the preserve, you will head south, joining an elevated trail through wetlands. The hike totals more than 9 miles so allow plenty of time to make the trek. Also, bring a hat sunscreen and plenty of water, as much of the trail is open overhead.

Distance: 9.8-mile loop
Hiking Time: 6.0 hours
Difficulty: Difficult due to distance
Highlights: Long hike, large land parcel
Cautions: Sun exposure, lack of water
Fees/Permits: No fees or permits required
Best Seasons: November through April
Other Trail Users: Equestrians. Leashed dogs allowed.
Trail Contacts: Prairie Pines Preserve, 18400 N. Tamiami Trail, North Fort Myers, FL 33903, (239) 533-8833, www.conservation2020.org
Finding the Trailhead: From exit 143 on I-75 north of Fort Myers, take Bayshore Road west for 5.3 miles to US 41 Business. Turn right, following US 41 Business for 2.4 miles, then merge north with US 41. Continue north for 1.4 miles; then look right for the turn into Prairie Pines Preserve.
GPS Trailhead Coordinates: N26° 43.939', W81° 54.537'

This hike explores a large parcel of land with miles and miles of trails. Prairie Pines Preserve was established not only to preserve a large tract of land for Lee County residents, but also to provide a significant aquifer recharge zone. In addition, since the eastern side of the park borders Interstate 75, and developed neighborhoods surround the 2,654-acre parcel, it seemed a natural acquisition. When purchased, the land was covered in melaleuca trees, but since the purchase, land stewards have been combining physical tree removal and prescribed fire to restore the ecosystem. Now you see pine flatwoods and wetland prairies that extend to the horizon. The visual effect of this is naturally eye-pleasing, but the proximity to I-75 keeps the sound of moving vehicles in your ears. However, plenty of wildlife call it home.

Sunrise among the evergreens at Prairie Pines Preserve.

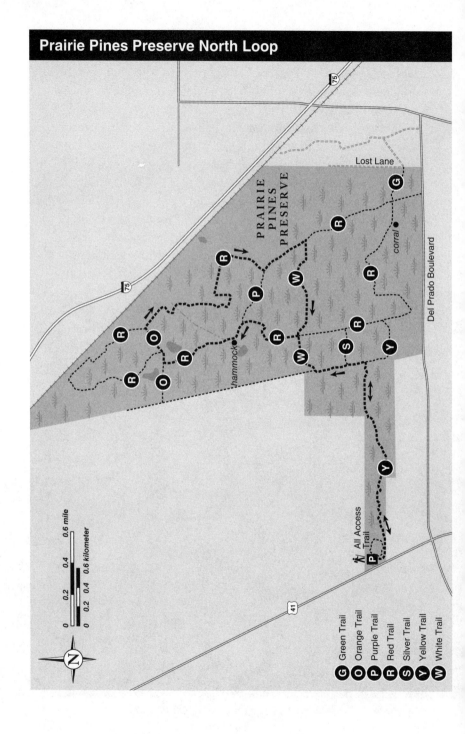

Prairie Pines Preserve North Loop

PRAIRIE PINES PRESERVE

Lost Lane

Del Prado Boulevard

corral

hammock

All Access Trail

0   0.2   0.4   0.6 mile
0   0.2   0.4   0.6 kilometer

N

G Green Trail
O Orange Trail
P Purple Trail
R Red Trail
S Silver Trail
Y Yellow Trail
W White Trail

The trail system uses color-coded metal posts to mark the trails. Permanent maps have been established at trail intersections, allowing you to keep apprised of your position. Make sure to pick up the Yellow Trail leaving from the large parking area. A hard-packed all-access trail makes a short half-mile loop but does not connect to the primary trail system.

The Yellow Trail quickly turns east, curving through tall pines with scattered palmetto squeezed into a narrow land parcel. Hikers can see housing on both sides of this parcel, but it does allow access to the main chunk of Prairie Pines Preserve. By 1.8 miles, you will cross a pair of canal bridges accessing the primary tract. Head left here, northbound, still on the Yellow Trail. The grassy doubletrack is bordered by palms, pines, and scrub oaks. The canal is off to your left. At 1.9 miles, meet the Silver Trail. It leaves right. Keep straight on the doubletrack path and join the White Trail at 2.2 miles. It curves easterly in thicker pines.

Reach the Red Trail and the loop portion of your hike at 2.5 miles. Turn left, northbound again, now on the Red Trail. Enjoy the long views with nothing but nature in the distance. Slash pines scatter over lower vegetation. You will see sporadic melaleuca trees, but they are being eradicated. At 3.1 miles, the Purple Trail leaves right and allows a shortcut. However, stay on the Red Trail to come alongside a hardwood hammock at 3.3 miles. Walk into the live oaks, palms, and lush vegetation for a cool, shady respite from the mostly open preserve.

The Red Trail keeps north, passing a wetland swale and willow thicket to meet the Orange Trail at 3.9 miles. Turn right here and follow it easterly to shortcut the Red Trail at 4.2 miles. Turn right, south, on the Red Trail. The path now goes off and on old roads, twisting and turning suddenly, and crosses a couple of shallow ditches. The correct route is well marked, however.

Watch for deer and hog tracks in the margins. You will also see old fences from cattle days. At 6.0 miles, reach the east end of the Purple Trail. Turn left here, joining an elevated berm that is sometimes sandy and open to the sun. At 6.5 miles, turn right onto the White Trail. Head westerly on this twisting path under prairie and pine to meet the Red Trail at 7.3 miles. You have completed the loop. From here it is a 2.5-mile backtrack to the trailhead.

Mileages at a Glance

0.0   Prairie Pines Preserve trailhead
1.8   Bridges
3.3   Hardwood hammock
3.9   Right on Orange Trail
6.5   Right on White Trail
7.3   Begin backtrack to trailhead
9.8   Return to trailhead

5

Prairie Pines Preserve South Loop

Hike Summary: This is the most popular long loop hike at Prairie Pines Preserve, a large tract of land near North Fort Myers. First, travel east along a piney corridor to begin the circuit. Cross a canal, then head clockwise through the lower portion of the preserve. You will walk through pine flatwoods along with more open seasonal wetland prairies. The latter part of the hike joins an elevated berm that keeps the footing dry year-round. Visit an old corral from cattle days, before continuing in mixed woodland to complete your loop.

Even the snakes like the trails here.

Distance: 8.0-mile loop
Hiking Time: 5.0 hours
Difficulty: Difficult due to distance
Highlights: Long hike, large land parcel
Cautions: Sun exposure, lack of water
Fees/Permits: No fees or permits required
Best Seasons: November through April
Other Trail Users: Equestrians. Leashed dogs allowed.
Trail Contacts: Prairie Pines Preserve, 18400 N. Tamiami Trail, North
   Fort Myers, FL 33903, (239) 533-8833, www.conservation2020.org
Finding the Trailhead: From exit 143 on I-75 north of Fort Myers, take
   Bayshore Road west for 5.3 miles to US 41 Business. Turn right, fol-
   lowing US 41 Business for 2.4 miles, then merge north with US 41.
   Continue north for 1.4 miles; then look right for the turn into Prairie
   Pines Preserve.
GPS Trailhead Coordinates: N26° 43.939', W81° 54.537'

This land was acquired through Lee County's Conservation
20/20 program. When acquired, the land was overrun with exotic melaleuca trees. However, the 2,654-acre tract, once ranch-
land, had potential. Since its acquisition, the property has been
transformed back to the naturally occurring ecosystems of
Southwest Florida. It takes a large piece of land to make a big
loop hike, and that is one advantage of Prairie Pines Preserve.
While here you might as well do a long hike, so strap on your
boots and get ready for a leg stretcher.

The multimile trail system uses color-coded metal posts to
mark the trails. They are open to horses, but equestrians seldom use the paths, except occasionally on weekends. Permanent
maps are posted at trail intersections, allowing you to keep apprised of your position. When leaving the parking area, don't
take the hard-packed all-access trail. It makes a short half-mile
loop but does not connect to the primary trail system.

Join the natural-surface Yellow Trail as it first heads south
and then east along a fence line. It soon begins a winding easterly course under swaying slash pines bordered by grasses and

Prairie Pines Preserve South Loop

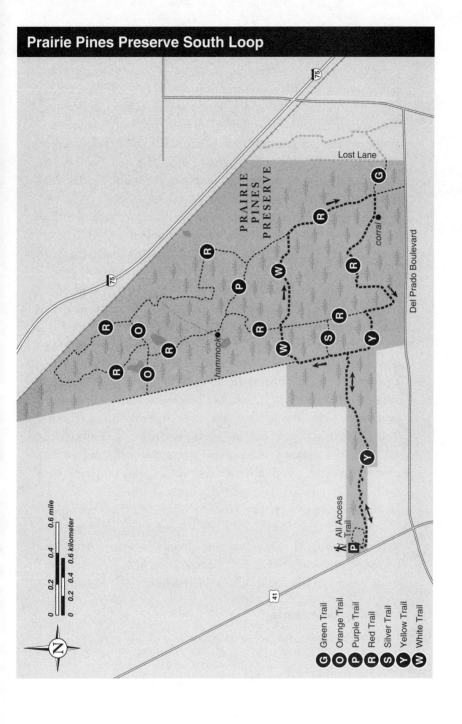

saw palmetto. The trail is hemmed in by neighborhoods to the north and south. This narrow corridor is used to access the main parcel of Prairie Pines Preserve. At 1.8 miles, come to a pair of canal bridges. Cross them and you have reached the primary tract. Head left here, northbound, still on the Yellow Trail, and begin your loop. The grassy doubletrack is bordered by palms, pines, and scrub oaks. The canal is off to your left. At 1.9 miles, come to the Silver Trail. It leaves right to meet the Red Trail. Keep straight on the doubletrack path and join the White Trail at 2.2 miles, which curves easterly in thicker pines.

Pass the Red Trail at 2.5 miles. Here, keep straight on the White Trail, traveling easterly on old roadbeds. Keep an eye peeled for the trail indicators here. At 3.4 miles, come to the Red Trail again. Turn right here, southbound on an elevated berm. Sections of the path can be sandy and are open to the sun, making for loose footing in places. Dense pines concentrate near the trail, but the corridor has been cleared of vegetation.

At 4.2 miles, reach a trail junction. Here the berm continues south toward Del Prado Boulevard, and the Green Trail heads east for Lost Lane. Turn right here, dropping off the berm but staying on the Red Trail, now heading westerly. Watch for old fence lines here. At 4.4 miles, pass the remains of an old corral. This was cattle country before it was encircled by civilization. Work around wetland swales ahead, grassy wetlands and willow domes. Pines vary in density. At 5.4 miles, the path approaches Del Prado Boulevard and then turns away.

Meet the Yellow Trail at 5.7 miles. Turn left here, resuming a westerly course. Come alongside a fence, marking the property boundary. The hike turns north near the main canal; then a grassy track leads to the loop's completion at 6.2 miles. From here, it is a 1.8-mile backtrack to the trailhead.

Mileages at a Glance

0.0 Prairie Pines Preserve trailhead
1.8 Bridges
2.2 Right on White Trail

3.4 Right on Red Trail
4.4 Pass an old corral
5.7 Left on Yellow Trail
6.2 Bridges
8.0 Return to trailhead

6

Caloosahatchee Creeks East Preserve

Hike Summary: This preserve, situated on the north shore of the Caloosahatchee River, presents three interconnected loops exploring a 1,300-acre tract of Southwest Florida plant communities. Though it doesn't reach the Caloosahatchee River, the hike does traverse varied woodlands, including a rich, junglelike swamp forest, dominated by regal cypresses. Also, explore live oak domes and pine flatwoods. The trailhead offers shaded picnic facilities, enhancing the experience.

Distance: 1.4-mile loop

Hiking Time: 1.0–1.5 hours

Difficulty: Easy

Highlights: Cypress-swamp boardwalk

Cautions: None

Fees/Permits: No fees or permits required

Best Seasons: Year-round

Other Trail Users: None. Leashed dogs allowed.

Trail Contacts: Lee County Parks & Recreation, 3410 Palm Beach Boulevard, Fort Myers, FL 33916, (239) 533-7275, www.leeparks.org

Finding the Trailhead: From exit 143 on I-75, northeast of Fort Myers, take FL 78 east for 1.1 miles to the preserve entrance on your right. Turn right into the preserve and follow it .2 mile to dead-end at the parking lot.

GPS Trailhead Coordinates: N26° 42.758', W81° 39.913'

Fern groves such as this add lushness to the forests of Southwest Florida.

Caloosahatchee Creeks East Preserve came to be as a result of Lee County's Conservation 20/20 program, which sprang up as a result of Lee County citizens wanting to set aside some of the county's alluring natural resources before they were gobbled up by homes and shopping centers. A county referendum was passed in order to purchase lands for the four following reasons: "Protect and preserve natural wildlife habitat, protect and preserve water quality and supply, protect developed lands from flooding and provide resource-based recreation." Conservation 20/20 is a smart, sensible plan that positively impacts Lee County residents.

The preserve lands were purchased over a four-year period for more than $8 million. Much of the land was disturbed and needed rehabilitation. Ditches, berms, dredge spoils from the river, and invasive flora and fauna compromised the expanse. Given time and refurbishment, however, the parcel has recovered nicely. Periodic fires and elimination of exotics, especially Brazilian pepper along streams, not only restore plant communities but also provide habitat for species such as gopher tortoise and downy woodpecker. Don't underestimate the importance of "protecting and preserving water quality." Not only do preserves such as this filter water, but they also provide aquifer recharge

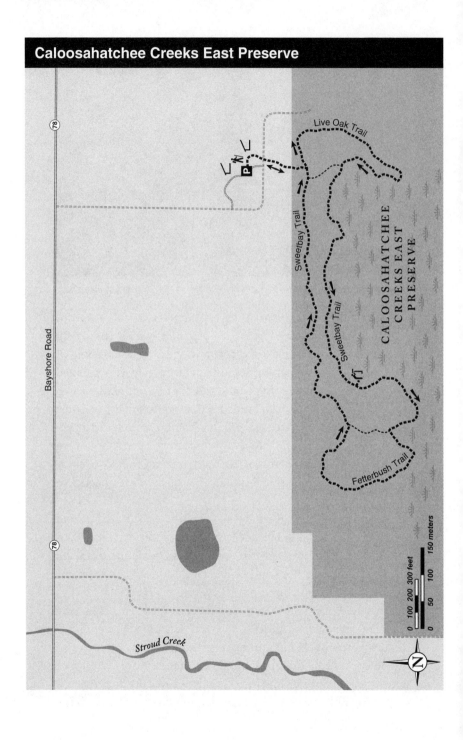

Caloosahatchee Creeks East Preserve

Live Oak Trail

Sweetbay Trail

Sweetbay Trail

Fetterbush Trail

CALOOSAHATCHEE CREEKS EAST PRESERVE

Bayshore Road

78

78

Stroud Creek

0 100 200 300 feet

0 50 100 150 meters

N

Scads of palms shade the inviting trail.

zones, allowing water to slowly soak into the soil rather than quickly running off paved surfaces. This slowing of water discharge also protects developed lands from being flooded. Finally, the preserve streams feed the Caloosahatchee River, the most important waterway in Southwest Florida.

The trailhead here is particularly attractive, set in live oak woods. The park presents sheltered picnic areas, shaded and sunny picnic areas, along with restrooms. Leave south from the trailhead, passing through a fence on the Live Oak Trail. Cross under a power line and then reenter woods. Here, take the Live Oak Trail left, easterly, on an all-access boardwalk overlain on the ground. Begin walking underneath live oaks with widestretched, shade-bearing limbs draped with Spanish moss and covered with resurrection ferns. The boardwalk elevates as it enters wetter terrain. At .3 mile, the Live Oak Trail meets the Sweetbay Trail. Turn left with the Sweetbay Trail, piercing deep into a wooded swamp.

Sweetbay, also known as swamp magnolia, is a part of the magnolia family, and grows in wet areas like this, along with cypresses, palms, and thick leatherferns. Sweetbay trees in Southwest Florida keep their leaves through the winter, despite being a deciduous tree. They display creamy white flowers in spring. From this vantage point, it is hard to imagine that decades ago here in Caloosahatchee Creeks East Preserve, the land was used for citrus and cattle. The park derives its name from six streams flowing through it to meet the Caloosahatchee River—Popash Creek, Stroud Creek, Palm Creek, Cohn Branch, Daughtreys Creek, and Chapel Branch. The creeks help form marshes, adding another plant community to the preserve. Other communities include sand live oaks, cabbage-palm forests, and pine flatwoods.

After tunneling through the swamp forest, the trail emerges alongside an open wetland at .6 mile. Here, an observation deck allows easterly marsh views. A water plant on the Caloosahatchee River rises in the distance. The Sweetbay Trail traverses the margin between the open wetland and the lush swamp forest. The boardwalk finally ends at .8 mile and you join a natural-surface trail. Just ahead, turn left and join the Fetterbush Trail. It leads through low-slung pine forest and brush, a palmetto prairie in places. This trail, open to the elements, contrasts with the dark swamp forest through which you walked earlier.

By 1.0 mile, the Fetterbush Trail is complete. Stay left, rejoining the Sweetbay Trail. The terrain is mostly forested now, though you pass through sandy, brushy, and grassy openings and among groves of sword ferns. These are native sword ferns, though non-native sword ferns are also now found in the Sunshine State. The warm climate of Southwest Florida invites a host of landscaping plants that inevitably escape and establish themselves in undesired places. Beyond the sword ferns, return to the Live Oak Trail at 1.4 miles. From here, it is but a short backtrack to the trailhead.

Mileages at a Glance

- 0.0 Caloosahatchee Creeks East Preserve Trailhead
- 0.3 Left on Sweetbay Trail
- 0.8 Left on Fetterbush Trail
- 1.0 Left on Sweetbay Trail
- 1.4 Left on Live Oak Trail, backtrack to trailhead

7

Telegraph Creek Preserve

Hike Summary: Enjoy exploring one of Lee County's newer nature preserves, located on Telegraph Creek, a tributary of the Caloosahatchee River. Start out in former cattle country and mixed forest. Come alongside Telegraph Creek before joining terrain that is more open and reach Bob Janes Preserve, yet another

Post-fire palmetto regenerates under a Southwest Florida sky.

Lee County natural property. Here, walk a mix of field and forest before returning to gain views of Telegraph Creek as it twists among cypress trees in a surprisingly deep channel. Finally, return to Telegraph Creek Preserve, making part of your return journey on an alternate route.

Distance: 4.1-mile figure-eight double loop
Hiking Time: 2.5 hours
Difficulty: Moderate
Highlights: Telegraph Creek
Cautions: Sun-exposed trail
Fees/Permits: No fees or permits required
Best Seasons: November through April
Other Trail Users: None. No dogs allowed.
Trail Contacts: Telegraph Creek Preserve, 18400 N. Tamiami Trail, North Fort Myers, FL 33903, (239) 533-8833, www.conservation2020.org
Finding the Trailhead: From exit 141 on I-75 near Fort Myers, take FL 80 east for 2.8 miles to FL 31. Turn left and take FL 31 north for 2.7 miles to County Road 78, North River Road. You will pass a left turn for 78 just after bridging the Caloosahatchee River. Ignore that left turn and keep forward on FL 31, passing the Lee County Civic Center; then turn right on CR 78, following it for 4.8 miles to the preserve entrance on your left.
GPS Trailhead Coordinates: N26° 43.733', W81° 41.351'

Lee County, in an attempt to conserve some of its natural beauty and recharge the underground aquifer serving the residents of Southwest Florida, continues to purchase and set aside strategic lands such as Telegraph Creek. This strategy serves the community well, offering passive recreation opportunities on lands that can soak in and filter the rains. This land also protects the banks of Telegraph Creek, allowing it to remain natural and wooded, so the stream, with its meanders and wooded bends, can handle high waters better than a straight-line canalized stream. Furthermore, the plants, animals, and aquatic creatures

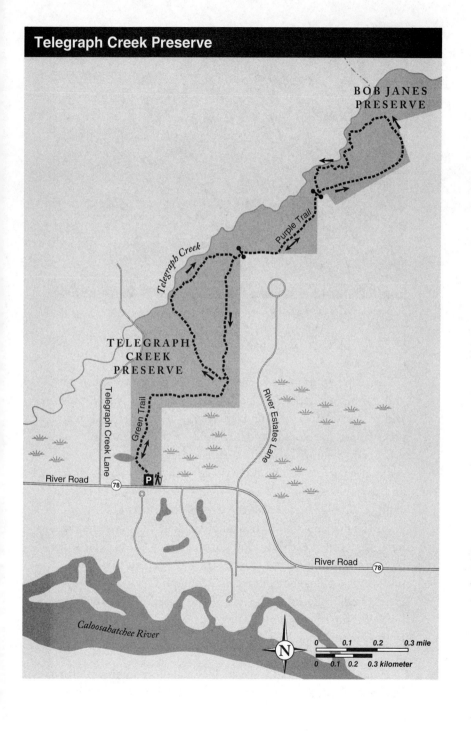

Telegraph Creek Preserve

BOB JANES
PRESERVE

Telegraph Creek

Purple Trail

TELEGRAPH
CREEK
PRESERVE

Telegraph Creek Lane

Green Trail

River Estates Lane

River Road   78

River Road   78

Caloosahatchee River

N

0   0.1   0.2   0.3 mile

0   0.1   0.2   0.3 kilometer

Streams such as this feed the Caloosahatchee River.

of Telegraph Creek will have a place to call home. It is a win all the way around.

Enter Telegraph Creek Preserve by passing through a gate and joining a doubletrack path amid wiregrass, palms, pines, and palmetto thickets. The trail system is marked with metal posts tipped in colored bands. You are on the Green Trail. Head northerly. The initial part of the preserve is narrow, and you can see houses across the boundary, especially in low-lying grassy and seasonal wetlands. Pass an old cattle-loading area to your right at .3 mile. Just ahead, the Green Trail turns easterly, as it enters a wider portion of the preserve. Live oaks line the track here. At .6 mile, reach the loop portion of the Green Trail. Turn left here, on a fainter but marked track. Begin cruising along an unnaturally widened tributary of Telegraph Creek. Piles of spoil create small hillocks to the left of the trail. This is exactly the kind of thing that nature preserves prevent. This occurred prior to the preserve purchase, and may be restored to a meandering stream down the line.

Come near Telegraph Creek. Live oaks predominate. Turn east, away from the stream at 1.2 miles. Reach a trail intersection and a meeting of properties. Here, the other end of the Green Trail comes in on your right. Save that for later. Instead, head left on a sandy fire road and then pass through a gate, entering Bob Janes Preserve. Here, resume east along a fence line, among tall pines, now tracing the Purple Trail.

At 1.4 miles, the Purple Trail leaves the fire road left, northeast, through pine/palmetto woodland. The Bob Janes Preserve was purchased from former Babcock Ranch holdings. At 1.6 miles, the Purple Trail turns north on a sand road. A large cattle-grazing meadow stretches to your right. Reach another gate at 1.7 miles. Cross this gate and enter lands open to cattle lease. You may see bovines roving about. Continue tracing the purple-tipped metal posts on the margin between meadow to your right and pineland to your left.

Turn left away from the prairie at 2.0 miles. Soon enter oak/palmetto thickets. At 2.1 miles, turn southwest, roughly paralleling Telegraph Creek. The path soon saddles alongside the slow, scenic stream popular with kayakers, especially closer to the Caloosahatchee River. Note its steep banks and cypress trees rising from the water's edge.

At 2.6 miles, you complete the loop within Bob Janes Preserve. Backtrack to Telegraph Creek Preserve and the Green Trail. From here, join new trail, southbound, at 3.0 miles. Pass through mostly open terrain. At 3.4 miles, reach a trail intersection. You have been here before. At this point, it is a simple backtrack to the trailhead.

Mileages at a Glance

- 0.0 Telegraph Creek Preserve trailhead
- 0.6 Reach loop portion of Green Trail
- 1.2 Enter Bob Janes Preserve, joining the Purple Trail
- 2.1 Saddle alongside Telegraph Creek
- 2.6 Complete loop on Purple Trail
- 3.0 Rejoin Green Trail, southbound
- 3.4 Complete loop of Green Trail, backtrack
- 4.0 Return to trailhead

8

Caloosahatchee Regional Park

Hike Summary: This is one of my personal favorite Southwest Florida hikes. This trek makes a wide loop through pines and deep into a riverside hardwood hammock, a dark and brooding jungle with huge live oaks flanked with palms, and a host of rich vegetation. Part of the circuit travels directly alongside the Caloosahatchee River, even stopping by a fishing pier for extensive aquatic views. The park also offers walk-in tent camping and kayaking.

Southwest Florida's preserves provide habitat for a whole range of wildlife, from turtles to bears.

Distance: 3.2-mile loop

Hiking Time: 2.0 hours

Difficulty: Moderate

Highlights: River views, tropical hardwood hammock

Cautions: None

Fees/Permits: Parking fee required

Best Seasons: November through April

Other Trail Users: None. No dogs allowed.

Trail Contacts: Lee County Parks and Recreation, 18500 North River Road, Alva, FL 33920, (239) 694-0398, www.leeparks.org

Finding the Trailhead: From exit 141 on I-75 near Fort Myers, take FL 80 east for 2.8 miles to FL 31. Turn left and take FL 31 north for 2.7 miles to County Road 78, North River Road. You'll pass a left turn for 78 just after bridging the Caloosahatchee River. Ignore that left turn and keep forward on FL 31, passing the Lee County Civic Center; then turn right on CR 78 and follow it for 7.0 miles to the main entrance on your right. The first park entrance will be the North Side Trails parking area, on the left; that is for the mountain-biking trails. Turn into the main entrance on the right and park.

GPS Trailhead Coordinates: N26° 43.337', W81° 39.125'

This recreation area on the shores of the Caloosahatchee River is one of Southwest Florida's finest. Not only does it have an alluring trail system, but it also has a great campground with excellent walk-in tent-camping sites. In addition to the hiking and camping, the park also presents paddling opportunities in the Caloosahatchee River and also nearby creeks that feed the river. Mountain bikers have an additional set of trails that they will find challenging; these are sometimes hiked as well.

This hike uses a collection of nature trails to tour the varied ecosystems of the park, from the piney uplands where gopher tortoises live, to tropical hardwood hammocks where giant live oaks spread their colossal limbs, and to an open shoreline, where the mighty Caloosahatchee River flows. As you face the park shelters at the trailhead, look right and take the Oxbow Trail leading northwest, away from the river, the trail closest to

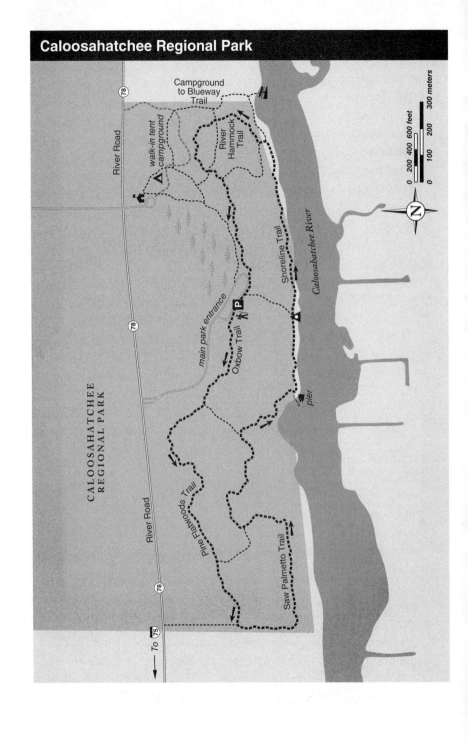

Caloosahatchee Regional Park

Campground to Blueway Trail

River Road

78

walk-in tent campground

River Hammock Trail

Shoreline Trail

Caloosahatchee River

main park entrance

P

Oxbow Trail

pier

CALOOSAHATCHEE REGIONAL PARK

River Road

Pine Flatwoods Trail

Saw Palmetto Trail

78

78

To 75

N

0   200   400   600 feet

0   100   200   300 meters

Eyeball-to-eyeball encounter with nature.

the entrance road. Begin hiking through a mixed forest of pines and scrub oaks. After a quarter mile, the Oxbow Trail leaves left, but you stay right, joining the Pine Flatwoods Trail. The sand, grass, and duff track wanders west, sometimes in scrub oaks, other times in pine flatwoods. At .7 mile, the path splits. Stay right with the outermost loop, now on the Saw Palmetto Trail. At .9 mile, reach the park's western boundary. Turn left here, aiming for the Caloosahatchee River. Hike south, paralleling an old ditch. At 1.1 miles, leave left from the ditch. The forest thickens—cypresses, live oaks, strangler figs, bay trees, and palms crowd the now-narrower track.

During the rainy season, many of these trails can be partly underwater. Avoid hiking here then. Turn away from the river in palms, meeting the Pine Flatwoods Trail at 1.4 miles. Turn right and continue hiking underneath a high-canopy tropical hammock, despite the trail name. Meet the Oxbow Trail at 1.7 miles and turn right here, aiming again for the Caloosahatchee. Soon the river opens into view and you reach a fishing pier that doubles as a river observation point.

Continue east, cruising along the shoreline in grass with scattered planted trees. You are walking atop dredge spoils from channel-deepening operations on the Caloosahatchee. Come to the wheelchair-accessible observation deck at 2.1 miles. It proffers additional river-viewing opportunities. Continue east along the river, still among planted trees and grasses, now on the Shoreline Trail. At 2.5 miles, turn left onto the River Hammock Trail—it makes a loop of its own. Go right as you reach the loop portion of the River Hammock Trail, getting into a nest of paths connecting to the campground. Stay with the River Hammock Trail; pass under mammoth old-growth live oaks, the size of which will amaze. You might get turned around a bit in this maze, but your wandering will be time well spent.

At 2.9 miles, come to the other end of the River Hammock Trail; stay right on the direct route back to the trailhead. Enjoy walking in hardwood hammock. You will see another path running parallel to you; this connects the campground to the trailhead. Emerge onto the parking area with its picnic shelters, water, and restrooms at 3.2 miles, completing your hike.

Mileages at a Glance

0.0   Caloosahatchee Park Main Entrance trailhead
0.9   Reach the park's western boundary
2.1   River observation deck
2.5   Begin River Hammock Trail
3.2   Return to trailhead

9

Hickeys Creek Mitigation Park

Hike Summary: This is one of the best and most unsung hikes in Southwest Florida. Walk a variety of landscapes, centered by alluring Hickeys Creek. First, hike pine flatwoods and then bridge Hickeys Creek, with its verdant riverine forest. Trek under tall oaks, pines, and open palmetto prairies before returning to the

The trail winds through a palmetto prairie framed in pines.

stream. Make a side loop, visiting a marsh, before returning to the trailhead in lush vegetation along Hickeys Creek.

Distance: 5.8-mile triple loop
Hiking Time: 3.5 hours
Difficulty: Moderate
Highlights: Hickeys Creek, multiple ecosystems
Cautions: None
Fees/Permits: Parking fee required
Best Seasons: Year-round
Other Trail Users: None. No dogs allowed.
Trail Contacts: Hickeys Creek Mitigation Park, 17980 Palm Beach Boulevard, Alva, FL 33920, (239) 694-0398, www.leeparks.org
Finding the Trailhead: From exit 141 on I-75, south of Fort Myers, take FL 80 east for 8.6 miles to reach Hickeys Creek Mitigation Park on your right.
GPS Trailhead Coordinates: N26° 42.758', W81° 39.913'

Hickeys Creek Mitigation Park is a jewel of the Lee County parks system. Located near the Caloosahatchee River, the park protects nearly 1,000 acres of the Hickeys Creek watershed. The preserve presents interconnected nature trails centered on Hickeys Creek, a picturesque tributary of the Caloosahatchee. I predict that once you make this hike, you will return and show a friend the fine scenery here.

Leave the trailhead, equipped with restrooms and water, then join the Hickeys Creek Trail, on an all-access path. The wide trail heads south through pine flatwoods and reaches an amphitheater alongside Hickeys Creek. Turn left, upstream along Hickeys Creek, and soon reach a spur trail leading to a fishing pier that allows great views of the silent stream. Pass a spur to a canoe/kayak launch; then cross the Live Oak Bridge over Hickeys Creek at .4 mile. The attractive waterway is bordered in live oaks and palms, along with scads of underbrush. Stay right, traveling boardwalk, still on Hickeys Creek Trail. Drop to a sandy

Hickeys Creek Mitigation Park

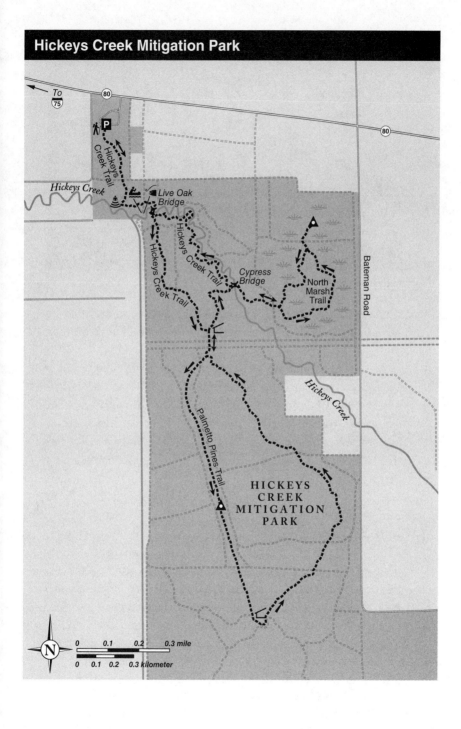

Author peers into Hickeys Creek.

singletrack, meandering north through tight young brush of scrub oaks and palmetto, heading toward the Palmetto Pines Trail.

At 1.0 mile, amid live oaks, turn right onto the Palmetto Pines Trail. Soon pass under a power line. The Palmetto Pines Trail next begins its loop—stay right here. Join an elevated berm overgrown with oaks, palms, and pines. The oak acorns attract pigs—you may see or hear some swine. Wild hogs are not native to Florida, or even the Americas, and are considered a pest threatening the Sunshine State's native flora and fauna. When Hernando de Soto first explored Florida, he brought hogs from Europe; some escaped and have been here ever since, breeding with other escaped swine. Wild hogs roam every Florida county, with an estimated half million in the state, despite heavy hunting pressure. Wild pigs not only feed on acorns and other mast, taking food from native fauna, but also raid farmer's crops and even prey on young, vulnerable livestock. What a pest!

Overgrown, often-moist ditches border the trail. At 1.6 miles, a wooden observation deck overlooks a pine-pocked palmetto prairie. Resume the southbound track. Leave the berm at 2.0 miles and curve sharply north, passing another rain shelter. Hike through the palmetto prairie you overlooked earlier. Also, cross occasional sand fire roads, where prescribed burns may leave the forest different from one side of the sand road to another. Keep meandering north.

Pines increase in number and density as you complete the Palmetto Pines Trail at 3.3 miles. Once again cross the power-line clearing, then stay right, rejoining the Hickeys Creek Trail. Come to another rain shelter, entering dense high-canopied forest of older pines, live oaks, and laurel oaks. At 3.5 miles, reach the Cypress Bridge. Turn right here on the North Marsh Trail, spanning a now much-smaller Hickeys Creek, though the vegetation remains verdant along the waterway. The slender footpath soon opens into classic pine flatwoods, with an understory of wiregrass and saw palmetto. At 3.7 miles, the path splits; stay right, making the North Marsh Trail circuit. Come near an old dug pond and spoil remnants. At 4.2 miles, join a spur trail leading right to the feature that gave the trail's name. Reach an elevated observation deck overlooking a seasonal pond. During winter and early spring the pond may be dead dry.

Backtrack to the North Marsh Trail, returning through pine flatwoods to reach the Cypress Bridge at 4.8 miles. Turn right, downstream along Hickeys Creek, back on the Hickeys Creek Trail. This is the best part of the hike. The singletrack trail meanders closely to the stream in tightly grown cypresses, palms, oaks, and ferns. The trail hastily twists and turns, mimicking a slalom course. You even have a little vertical variation. Return to the Live Oak Bridge at 5.4 miles. Now it is a matter of backtracking to the trailhead, completing the hike at 5.8 miles.

Mileages at a Glance

- 0.0 Hickeys Creek Mitigation Park trailhead
- 0.4 Cross the Live Oak Bridge over Hickeys Creek
- 1.0 Right on Palmetto Pines Trail
- 3.3 Complete the loop portion of Palmetto Pines Trail
- 3.7 Begin North Marsh Trail circuit
- 4.8 Complete North Marsh Trail circuit
- 5.4 Cross the Live Oak Bridge
- 5.8 Return to trailhead

Pine Island Flatwoods Preserve

Hike Summary: Take a short ramble through the woodland for which Pine Island was named. From the parking area, a trail wanders through well-restored native pine flatwoods. It then begins a circuit, crossing sandy fire roads, which can extend your hike. Enjoy sweeps of slash pines lording over stark flats of palmetto before completing the trek.

Hiking through native pine flatwoods that once covered much of Florida.

Distance: 1.4-mile loop
Hiking Time: 1.0 hours
Difficulty: Easy
Highlights: Exemplary pine flatwoods community
Cautions: Sun exposure
Fees/Permits: No fees or permits required
Best Seasons: Year-round
Other Trail Users: None. No dogs allowed.
Trail contacts: Calusa Land Trust, PO Box 216, Bokeelia, FL 33922, www.
   calusalandtrust.org. No telephone.
Finding the Trailhead: From the intersection of US 41 and Lee County
   78 in North Fort Myers, take Lee County 78 west across Cape Coral
   for a total of 15.0 miles. Reach Pine Island and a four-way intersec-
   tion. Turn left here on Lee County 767 south, Stringfellow Road, and
   follow it 4.5 miles to reach the preserve on your right.
GPS Trailhead Coordinates: N26° 33.111', W82° 5.569'

I wish this hike were a little longer. It is 1.4 miles in length, but
the preserve size could handle many more miles of trails. Visitors would be well served if that were the case. However, you
can incorporate the fire roads lacing the preserve into additional
hiking mileage. The preserve harbors a surprisingly large swath
of Pine Island, one of Southwest Florida's largest islands. Pine
Island still has a touch of the slow life, with agriculture still
hanging on in places (including near the preserve) versus other
islands such as Estero or Sanibel that are developed out. Eleva-
tions of the preserve range from 8 feet at its highest in the pines
to 2 feet in the salt flats and tidal waters in its southwest corner.

This lack of high-pressure development made purchasing the
Pine Island Flatwoods Preserve property easier for Lee County,
which purchased the property in 2002. This tract is comanaged
with the Calusa Land Trust, in operation since 1976. As you walk
through the preserve, note the archetypal nature of the pine flatwoods. Like most of Florida's native ecosystems, pine flatwoods
need fire to maintain their character. Otherwise oaks and other
hardwoods will crowd out the pines and palmettos. Fire has been
used here, and you will see its evidence throughout the preserve.

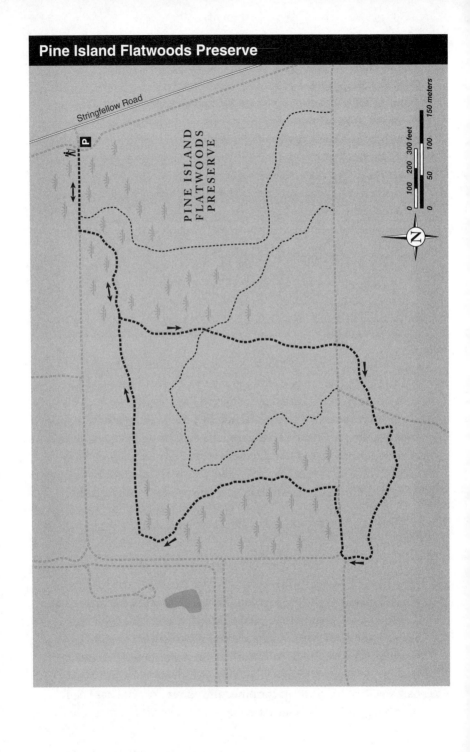

Pine Island Flatwoods Preserve

Past uses of the land include citrus production, a shrimp farm, and cattle pasturage. Its 635 acres were acquired in five tracts for over $5 million. It is mostly in its original state, especially the tidal swamp, which includes 100 acres. However, the pine flatwoods, comprising 415 acres, were timbered in the early 1900s, taking old-growth longleaf pines. Exotic melaleuca trees had made inroads prior to purchase, but have since been removed. The rest of the park's acreage houses other plant communities such as depression marsh and coastal grasslands.

Leave the small parking area and enter the underutilized preserve on the one and only marked hiking trail. Posts with a hiker symbol blazed in green designate the path. Wiregrass, palmetto, and the occasional palm tree complement the slash and longleaf pines scattered over the landscape. At .1 mile, the Green Trail splits left off a fire road it has been tracing. The trail bed narrows as it makes a serpentine route through palmetto.

At .2 mile, reach the loop portion of the hike. Stay left here, heading south. Cross a fire road at .4 mile. As is often the case, fire roads delineate prescribed burn zones, so simply stepping across a sandy lane will take you into a different-age pine forest, or one that has been recently burned, or not recently burned. The forests may not even be different ages, but one might be thick with brush (no recent burning) and the other more open (recent burning). Cross more fire lanes ahead. If you choose to strike out on these fire lanes, be apprised they are sandy in places and can be slow going.

The loop turns back north to enter more open prairie. Come very near private property before aiming for the trailhead. Finish the circuit at 1.2 miles; then it is a .2 mile backtrack to the trailhead.

Mileages at a Glance

0.0   Pine Island Flatwoods Preserve trailhead
0.2   Begin loop portion of hike, heading left, westerly
1.2   Complete the loop
1.4   Return to trailhead

11

Four Mile Cove Ecological Preserve

Hike Summary: Explore the lower Caloosahatchee River at this Cape Coral preserve. Tunnel into a mangrove forest, mostly on boardwalk. The elevated walkway then takes a there-and-back trip to a pond, then turns to the shore of Four Mile Cove, where a pier extends into the water, availing stellar views. Finally, the trail leads to another pier and a farther-ranging vista. Close the loop with a trek through maritime hardwoods.

Distance: 1.7-mile loop
Hiking Time: 1.5 hours
Difficulty: Easy
Highlights: Wide Caloosahatchee River views, mangrove boardwalk
Cautions: None
Fees/Permits: No fees or permits required
Best Seasons: November through April
Other Trail Users: None. No dogs allowed.
Trail Contacts: Four Mile Cove Ecological Preserve, SE 23rd Terrace, Cape Coral, FL 33990, (239) 549-4606, www.capecoral.net
Finding the Trailhead: From exit 136 on I-75 south of Fort Myers, take Colonial Parkway west for 8.8 miles, bridging the Caloosahatchee River and entering Cape Coral, where the road becomes Veterans Memorial Parkway. Just after the bridge toll booth, turn right at the sign for SE 17th Terrace. Drive a very short distance and then turn right again onto SE 23rd Terrace and follow SE 23rd Terrace a mile to the trailhead, at a dead end. The trail starts on the left.
GPS Trailhead Coordinates: N26° 36.501', W81° 55.123'

A view into Four Mile Cove.

The city of Cape Coral is a vast array of streets, canals, and development that many Southwest Floridians call home. Recreation and preservation are also components of a successful community. Four Mile Cove Ecological Preserve provides such a thing. It makes available an oasis of wildness for the mangrove forests and maritime woodlands bordering the Caloosahatchee River, the watery artery of Southwest Florida that links Lake Okeechobee to the Gulf of Mexico. Cape Coral Parks and Recreation has developed a boardwalk traversing incredibly dense and interesting mangrove thickets located in the 365-acre preserve. For good measure, the boardwalk also opens to the water's edge, where you can see the nexus of land and river, along with plenty of civilization, adding an exclamation point onto the importance of this park.

Four Mile Cove Ecological Preserve

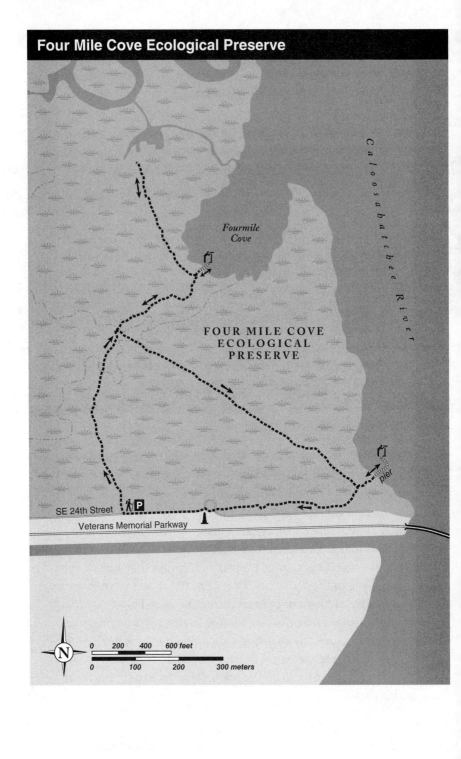

Caloosahatchee River

Fourmile Cove

FOUR MILE COVE
ECOLOGICAL
PRESERVE

pier

SE 24th Street

P

Veterans Memorial Parkway

N

0   200   400   600 feet

0   100   200   300 meters

The Veterans Memorial rises against the Southwest Florida winter sky.

Facing the preserve, look left, or westerly, for a kiosk and walkway leaving north from the parking area. Immediately dip into mangrove forest. Leatherfern finds a home in the intertwined trunks and roots of the evergreens. The elevated trail heads through a tunnel of growth, where the three types of mangrove—white, red, and black—are represented. Florida is home to the world's largest mangroves, situated in Everglades National Park to the south. Of the three mangroves, red mangroves are easiest to identify. They have smooth, green, waxy evergreen leaves sprouting from an off-white trunk. Near the base of the tree sprout what are known as prop roots—curved roots extending from the main trunk into the water below. Oysters and other marine life cling to the roots. The function of these roots is unclear. They have been thought to help stabilize the tree by trapping sediments around the roots, to help the tree "breathe" due to its tidal inundations, or to leach out the salt from the sea. Red mangroves are the most salt-tolerant mangrove. The tidal shallows in and around red mangroves act as nurseries, breeding and feeding grounds for estuarine plants and animals, from shrimp to snapper to shorebirds.

At .3 mile, the boardwalk splits. Stay left here toward Four Mile Cove. Bridge a tidal stream that pushes back and forth with the cycles of the moon. Continue passing widened areas of the boardwalk, replete with benches and interpretive information, places where you can learn and relax. At .4 mile, stay left again, as the boardwalk leading right heads to a view of Four Mile Cove. For now, continue walking in the mangrove maze, to reach a dead end near Lost Pond, at .6 mile. Lost Pond is often accessed using kayaks, which can be rented at the preserve from November through April.

Backtrack again to reach the viewing deck of Four Mile Cove at .8 mile. Step out here, absorbing the river-framed vista of the cove and the more open expanse of the wide Caloosahatchee River. Look below at the clear waters of the cove, as well as the reddish aqua in the mangrove channels. At 1.0 mile, turn left, rejoining the main loop and traveling more boardwalks. Although the hike remains shady, it is not recommended for summer hiking as the mosquitoes may be troublesome in the mangrove. At 1.4 miles, split left, coming to another open observation pier. You are now looking at the extremely wide Caloosahatchee River, bay-like at this point, since it is so near to its mouth at the Gulf of Mexico.

Beyond here, the hike leaves the boardwalk, joining land. Enter a coastal hammock forest, rich with royal palms, sea grapes, and oaks. Come to the eastern edge of the parking lot. Reach the Veterans Memorial area, where erected monuments memorialize soldiers from several wars. The tributes, overlooking Veterans Memorial Parkway, can be seen from the trailhead and the adjacent road.

Mileages at a Glance

0.0   Four Mile Cove Park trailhead
0.6   Turn around at Lost Pond
1.0   Rejoin main loop
1.4   Observation pier overlooking Caloosahatchee River
1.7   Return to trailhead

12

Calusa Nature Center

Hike Summary: This is a great place for kids, young and old. Enjoy a comprehensive museum with its exhibits; view the raptors at the bird aviary and smaller winged creatures at the butterfly aviary. Next, traverse a boardwalk through swamp forest, then take off to the lesser-visited parcel, hiking through a multitude of habitats. Finally, an elevated berm returns you to the museum.

The bird aviary allows visitors to see rescued birds up close.

Distance: 1.9-mile loop

Hiking Time: 1.5 hours

Difficulty: Easy

Highlights: Bird aviary, cypress boardwalk

Cautions: Limited hours: 10 a.m. to 5 p.m., Monday-Saturday; 11 a.m. to 5 p.m. Sunday

Fees/Permits: Entrance fee required

Best Seasons: Year-round

Other Trail Users: None. No dogs allowed.

Trail Contacts: Calusa Nature Center, 3450 Ortiz Avenue, Fort Myers, FL 33905, (239) 275-3435, www.calusanature.org

Finding the Trailhead: From exit 136 on I-75 in Fort Myers, take Colonial Boulevard west for .4 mile to a traffic light at Ortiz. Turn right on Ortiz (the left turn will be Six Mile Cypress Boulevard) and follow Ortiz .2 mile to turn left into the Calusa Nature Center.

GPS Trailhead Coordinates: N26° 36.950', W81° 48.747'

This privately run operation is an oasis of wildness in Fort Myers. It not only offers hiking trails, but also has a museum displaying Southwest Florida human and natural history. The center's planetarium is also a big draw. Your entrance fee covers admittance to all the above, making your hike just part of an enjoyable day at this natural destination.

To reach the trails, make your way through the museum, paying your fee while inside. Emerge from the museum, visiting the butterfly aviary. The Calusa Nature Center has been caring for injured birds for decades. The ones you see cannot make it in the wild after their setbacks. Pick up the Cypress Loop, following the numbered stops and interpretive information clockwise. Ramble through a mixed woodland, not entirely swamp yet not entirely upland either, a blend of pine, palm, cypress, and palmetto.

At .1 mile, the Pine Loop leaves right. Stay straight with the Cypress Loop Trail. Pass the first of several rain/sun shelters situated along the trail. Enjoy interpretive information as you stroll along. At .2 mile, join the boardwalk as it enters deep cypress forest and seasonal wetlands. The boardwalk makes several

Calusa Nature Center

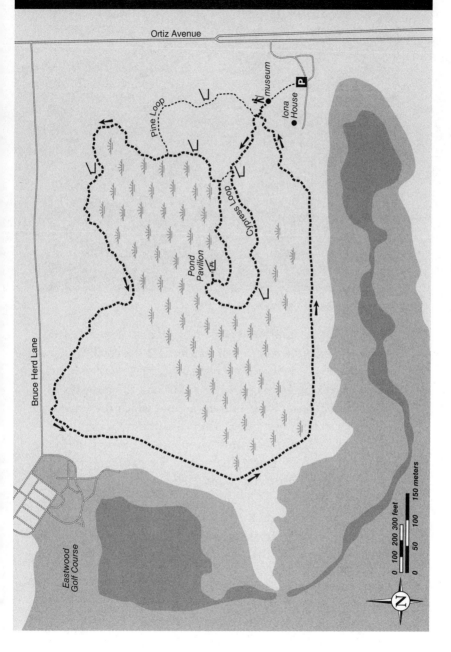

This is what you call the ol' eagle eye.

surprising twists and turns while meandering among the watery woodland. At .4 mile, a spur trail leads to the Pond Pavilion. Here, you can overlook an open pond bordered by swamp forest. This is a favorable birding location. Continue along the boardwalk, passing beside cypress trees around which the walkway was constructed. Majestic royal palms rise from adjacent terrain.

At .5 mile, the boardwalk ends. Keep forward, joining the Pine Loop, as a shortcut leads right, back to the nature center. The natural-surface path travels amid saw palmetto, cypress, and pine. Saw palmetto often snakes along the surface of woodlands. It is found in the understory of Florida's forests, especially piney woods, from poorly drained flatwoods to rolling sand pine scrub forests. Its range stretches beyond the bounds of the Sunshine State into southeasternmost South Carolina west to southern Mississippi. Their spiny fronds are similar to those of sabal palm. Florida panthers often den in its thickets. Wild turkeys nest among them, and deer hide in copses of the low-growing plant.

Like many plants in Florida, saw palmetto is positively affected by fire. Its trunk can withstand a burning and its fronds come back strong and grow rapidly after burning. It also flowers and fruits more abundantly following a burn. Saw-palmetto berries are an important food source for everything from opossums to deer to bears. Aboriginal Floridians such as the Calusa counted saw-palmetto berries as a staple of their diet. Today, extract of saw palmetto is taken as medicine for prostrate problems, though many believe this is another unproven health fad.

At .6 mile, leave the main nature-trail network, staying left with the Wildlands Trail. You are now going to explore the "back 40" of the 105-acre preserve. Laurel oak, cypress, pine, and sawgrass form the trailside vegetation. The path becomes a slender singletrack. Pass a trail shelter at .8 mile. Turn westerly. At 1.1 miles, come near Eastwood Golf Course. It looks as if the trail is going to reach the road lying between you and the golf course, but it suddenly turns left and picks up an elevated berm.

Make a southerly track in thick woods bordered by a vegetated ditch. The hard-packed path makes for easy hiking. At 1.5 miles, the trail turns east. Look off the berm. Note the underlying pinnacle rock, exposed to dig fill to make this berm. At 1.8 miles, the trail drops left off the berm onto steps. Shortly come to the main outbuildings of the nature center. Soon return to the museum, completing the loop.

Mileages at a Glance

0.0 Calusa Nature Center trailhead
0.2 Join the Cypress Loop boardwalk
0.6 Join the Wildlands Trail
1.1 Come near a golf course
1.5 Trail turns east
1.9 Return to trailhead

13

Six Mile Cypress Slough Preserve

Hike Summary: You will appreciate this boardwalk that makes a circuit through a gorgeous preserved wetland. Start by crossing a thick cypress copse; then come to Gator Lake. Cruise along the shore of this open water before turning into a deep, wooded swamp. Walk among pop ash, cypress, ferns, bromeliads, and other tropical vegetation of the rich aquatic forest. The board- walk then cruises by a smaller pond favored by birds. You will

Looking out on Gator Lake.

continue in deep swamp woodland, making one last side trip by another birding deck. Take time to visit the environmental center while you are here.

Distance: 1.2-mile loop
Hiking Time: 1.0 hours
Difficulty: Easy
Highlights: Swamp forest, birding, environmental education
Cautions: None
Fees/Permits: Parking permit required
Best Seasons: Year-round
Other Trail Users: None. No dogs allowed.
Trail Contacts: Lee County Parks & Recreation, 3410 Palm Beach Blvd.
  Fort Myers, FL 33916, (239) 533-7275, www.leeparks.org
Finding the Trailhead: From exit 136 on I-75 south of Fort Myers, take
  FL 884, Colonial Boulevard west for .3 mile to a light. Turn left on
  Six Mile Cypress Road (the right turn is Ortiz Road), and follow it
  3.2 miles to Penzance Boulevard and enter Six Mile Cypress Slough
  Preserve. The trail starts in the upper parking area, away from the
  environmental center.
GPS Trailhead Coordinates: N26° 34.2775', W81° 49.5654'

Six Mile Cypress Slough, situated south and east of Fort Myers, is an important part of the aquifer puzzle for Southwest Florida. This channel of slow-moving water flows southwesterly toward Estero Bay. Six Mile Cypress Slough, which is nine miles in length, totaling 2,500 acres, is nearly encircled by development. The fact that it has not been turned into houses or shopping centers is a testament to its wetland state. Over time, citizens have realized that it is smart to preserve places like Six Mile Cypress Slough, not only for the plant and animal life within, but also for the aquifer recharge zones they provide. Furthermore, this preserve offers visitors environmental education in addition to the opportunity to appreciate the preserve's natural features, namely the deep-woods cypress swamp.

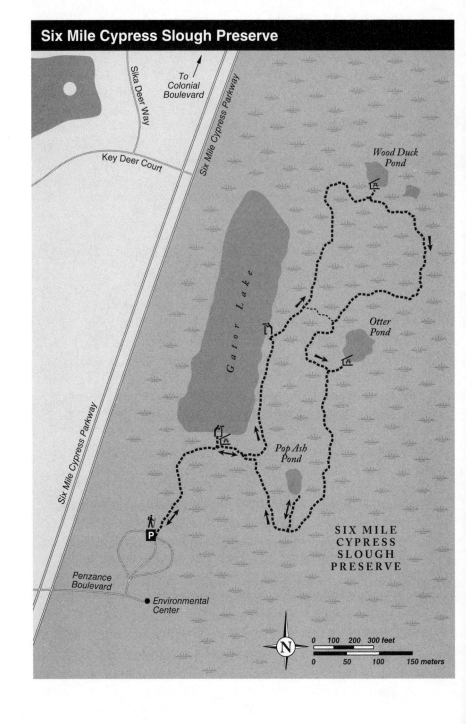

Six Mile Cypress Slough Preserve

Sika Deer Way

To Colonial Boulevard

Six Mile Cypress Parkway

Key Deer Court

Wood Duck Pond

Gator Lake

Otter Pond

Pop Ash Pond

Six Mile Cypress Parkway

SIX MILE CYPRESS SLOUGH PRESERVE

Penzance Boulevard

Environmental Center

0   100   200   300 feet

N

0   50   100   150 meters

Avian life is abundant in Six Mile Cypress Slough.

The trailhead presents shaded picnic areas, restrooms, and water. Before or after your walk make sure to visit the environmental education center, where you can learn more about this preserve. Guided hikes are regularly led here; they are a good way to learn about the flora and fauna of Six Mile Cypress Slough. Start your hike at the shaded kiosk and then pick up a boardwalk, which immediately traverses a collection of cypress trees rising from a seasonal wetland. Although this is a watery destination, mosquitoes aren't much of a problem here, making the preserve a year-round destination. The forest thickens as you enter drier woods of oaks, pines, and willows. Soon reach a gazebo displaying information about the slough, as well as a spur trail leading to an observation deck overlooking Gator Lake. You may see birds or alligators in season.

At .2 mile, begin the loop portion of the hike, heading left along the east shore of Gator Lake. The squarish shape of the lake is a giveaway that Gator Lake is not natural. The impoundment was created when fill was dredged for material to build up nearby Six Mile Cypress Parkway. Laurel oaks, maples, and palms border the path. Pass one more observation deck before leaving Gator Lake. The platforms you see in the lake are "floating habitats" designed to attract wildlife, which in turn can be viewed by visitors.

Soon enter a gorgeous hardwood tropical swamp forest. The junglelike setting presents a primeval aspect—Spanish moss draped over trees, resurrection ferns, queer cypress knees, splayed bromeliads, squawking birds, the amalgam of dark water and land. At .3 mile, a shortcut leaves right; keep straight through more swamp woods. At .5 mile, a short spur leads left to the Wood Duck Pond. Here you can view waterfowl and other aquatic life.

The boardwalk then turns south, nearing some big and impressive cypresses. Pass a shortcut and reach another observation deck, this one overlooking Otter Pond. At 1.0 mile, take a longer spur leading to Pop Ash Pond. This overlook is equipped with a viewing blind, increasing your chances of viewing birds without disturbing them. This is a popular place for photographers and bird-watchers with binoculars. Backtrack to the main loop and you quickly reach the south end of Gator Lake. From here it is but a simple backtrack to the trailhead.

Mileages at a Glance

0.0 Six Mile Cypress Slough Preserve trailhead
0.1 Reach Gator Lake, left at trail split
0.3 Wood Duck Pond
1.0 Spur to Pop Ash Pond
1.2 Return to trailhead

14

Wild Turkey Strand Preserve

Hike Summary: Combine history and hiking at this newer Lee County preserve, once the site of a World War II training facility. Take the Gunner Trail through gorgeous restored pine/palmetto forest before visiting a wetland overlook, with birds in season. From there, travel boardwalks past more wetlands and prairies. Come to outbuildings left over from the days when this locale was an army base, training gunners. The final part of the hike loops among more pines, reaching the trailhead.

Distance: 1.8-mile loop
Hiking Time: 2.0 hours, including stops at interpretive stations
Difficulty: Easy
Highlights: U.S. Air Force base relics
Cautions: Sun exposure
Fees/Permits: No fees or permits required
Best Seasons: November through April
Other Trail Users: None. No dogs allowed.
Trail Contacts: Wild Turkey Strand Preserve, 18400 N. Tamiami Trail, North Fort Myers, FL 33903, (239) 533-8833, www.conservation2020. org
Finding the Trailhead: From exit 138 on I-75, take FL 82 east for 8.1 miles to turn right on Rod & Gun Club Road. Follow Rod & Gun Club Road just a short distance; then turn left into the preserve entrance. Follow the entrance road to dead end in a loop. The Gunner Trail starts here.
GPS Trailhead Coordinates: N26° 42.758', W81° 39.913'

Wild Turkey Strand Preserve

Meadow Road

Old SR 82

82

82

Rod and Gun Club Road

P

gun turret
foundation

munitions
building

munitions
building

Gunner Trail

WILD TURKEY
STRAND
PRESERVE

N

| 0 | 200 | 400 | 600 feet |

| 0 | 100 | 200 | 300 meters |

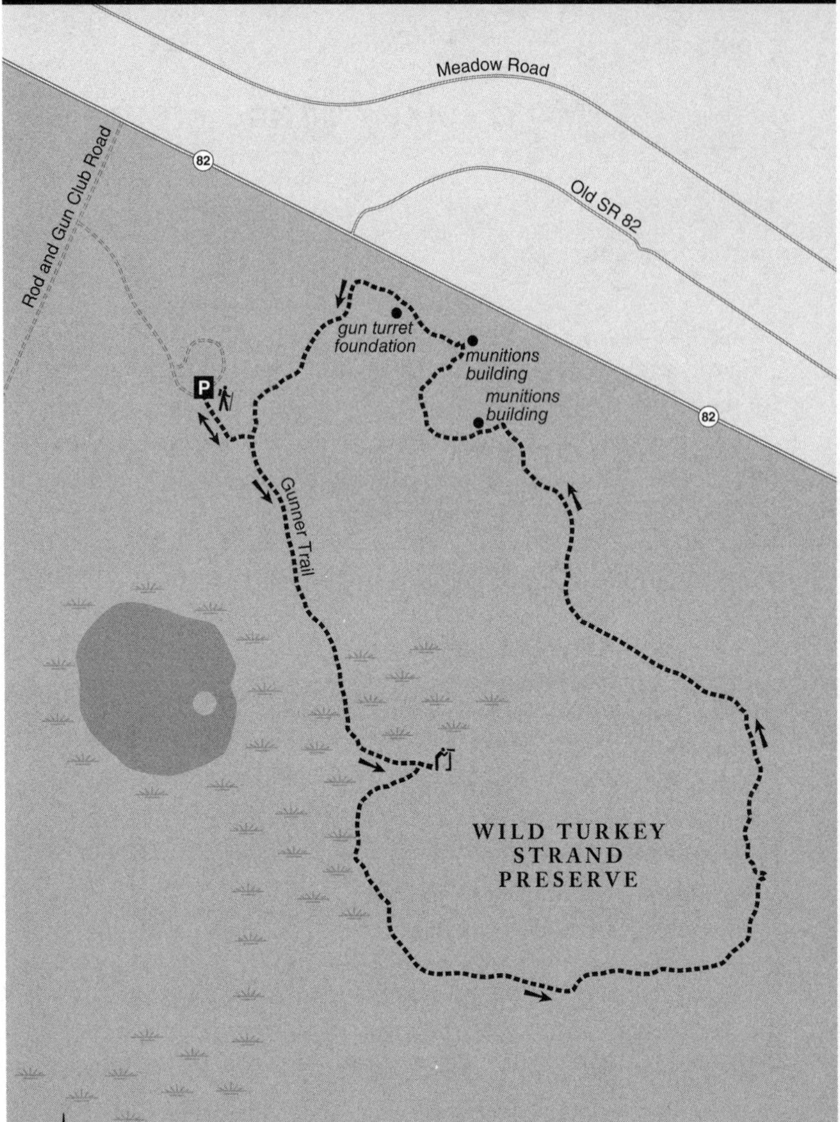

Leftover munitions building.

When World War II erupted, American armed forces mobilized in myriad ways. Here in Southwest Florida, Buckingham Army Air Field was created in 1942, including a gunnery school, on 50,000 acres. Gunners rode on bomber planes that shot at the enemy from Europe to the Pacific Ocean. During Buckingham's three-year life, thousands of gunners were trained. The area was deactivated in 1945. Salvageable items were moved to other locations. Scavengers combed over the area, leaving surprisingly scant evidence as to what transpired during that one-thousand-day period. Today, it stands as a natural area, interspersed with relics from the days when soldiers trained and lived here in what was then remote Southwest Florida. Today, the Gunners Trail explores not only relics such as a munitions building, but also the natural landscape that continues to thrive under the auspices of Lee County's Conservation 20/20 program.

The trailhead offers a shaded picnic shelter, water pump, and restroom. Take the Gunners Trail, marked in quarter-mile increments, on a walkway called flexi-pave. Much of the material used in its manufacture was recycled. Walk among prototype pine/palmetto forest, where green and tan thickets of low-slung fan-shaped leaves surge from the ground-running trunks of palmetto. Above that soar the broken-barked bronze trunks of slash pines, topped with slender green needles. Traces of black, reminders of prescribed burns, partially color the bases of both the pine and palmetto.

Quickly reach the loop portion of the hike. Head right, counterclockwise. Join a boardwalk. Open onto a wiregrass prairie, wet in the summer and mostly dry in the winter. Pine copses and cypress domes rise in the distance. At .4 mile, reach an observation platform overlooking a willow pond, holding water throughout the year. Expect to see wood storks and other avian life. Drop off the boardwalk, curving south in oak/palmetto scrub, alternating with grasses and willow thickets.

At .9 mile, reach a second observation platform, overlooking still more seasonal wetlands. Binoculars would come in handy here. Resume the loop north, now on an extended boardwalk over more marsh. Just the slight elevation of the boardwalk extends your panoramas of this 3,100-acre preserve, one of the largest in the Conservation 20/20 system. It was acquired in three tracts in the early 2000s. By 2008, habitat restoration was under way, and it was opened in early 2013. Expect the trail system to expand. Instead of a natural area, imagine it as part of an army base in days gone by. The recuperative powers of nature can be amazing, yet ahead you will literally see concrete evidence of the past.

At 1.4 miles, reach the first munitions building, built into a mound. The rectangular concrete structure once housed ammo. Circle around a marsh created from the extraction of fill; then come to the second munitions building at 1.5 miles. You are near FL Highway 82. Join a paved surface and then pass some concrete gunnery works, including concrete bases. Most of the old military installation was salvaged. Why the two buildings and concrete turret bases were left is now lost to time. However, thanks to Lee County's Conservation 20/20 program, places like Wild Turkey Strand Preserve are being held for future generations to enjoy. The hike turns toward the trailhead, passing through pine scrub before completing the circuit. A short backtrack leads to the trailhead, and your arrival at 1.8 miles.

Mileages at a Glance

0.0 Wild Turkey Strand Preserve trailhead
0.4 Reach first observation platform
0.9 Reach second observation platform
1.4 First munitions building
1.5 Second munitions building
1.8 Complete the Gunner Trail

15

Tram Trail

Hike Summary: Take a sun-splashed hike atop an old logging tram road at Okaloacoochee Slough State Forest. The raised track borders wetlands and provides a chance to view the surrounding state forest. Your return route, on Sic Island Road, makes an easy path, bisecting more wetlands in Florida's "Big Sky Country." On your way to the trailhead, take a short, palm-bordered nature walk overlooking Okaloacoochee Slough, then add a meal at the shaded picnic area, near the Tram Trail parking area.

Okaloacoochee Slough is part of Southwest Florida's Big Sky Country.

Distance: 3.6-mile loop

Hiking Time: 3.0 hours

Difficulty: Moderate

Highlights: Views from old logging railroad, open wetland vistas, solitude

Cautions: Sun exposure

Fees/Permits: No fees or permits required

Best Seasons: Year-round, check hunting dates

Other Trail Users: None. Leashed dogs allowed.

Trail Contacts: Okaloacoochee Slough State Forest, 6265 County Road 832, Felda, FL 33930, (863) 612-0776, www.floridaforestservice.com

Finding the Trailhead: From the intersection of FL 29 and FL 82, east of Fort Myers and north of Immokalee, take FL 29 north for 7.6 miles, then turn right onto Hendry County 832. Follow 832 east for 3.8 miles to Sic Island Road. Turn right on Sic Island Road, first reaching the boardwalk at .1 mile on the left. To reach the Tram Trail, keep forward on Sic Island Road for .7 mile, just after passing the state forest picnic area on your left.

GPS Trailhead Coordinates: N26° 35.395', W81° 22.710'

On your way to the main hike, make sure to stop at the boardwalk just after turning onto Sic Island Road. This short trail meanders through an alluring palm forest before reaching a boardwalk that rises to an overlook of Okaloacoochee Slough. Here, you can see the vegetated wetlands running north-south through the state forest. This slow sheet flow is part of the greater Everglades ecosystem and is still in its pre-Columbian state, unlike most parts of the Everglades today, which have been canalized, dredged, or otherwise altered.

Since the Tram Trail is elevated throughout, it can be hiked at any time of year, though most of the hunting at this state forest is done on fall weekends. From the trailhead, Sic Island Road goes left and the hiker-only Tram Trail leaves right. Trace an elevated berm among palms, willows, and wiregrass. At .1 mile, reach a chain gate and an old railroad grade. This railroad grade gave the Tram Trail its name. Railroad lines built for logging

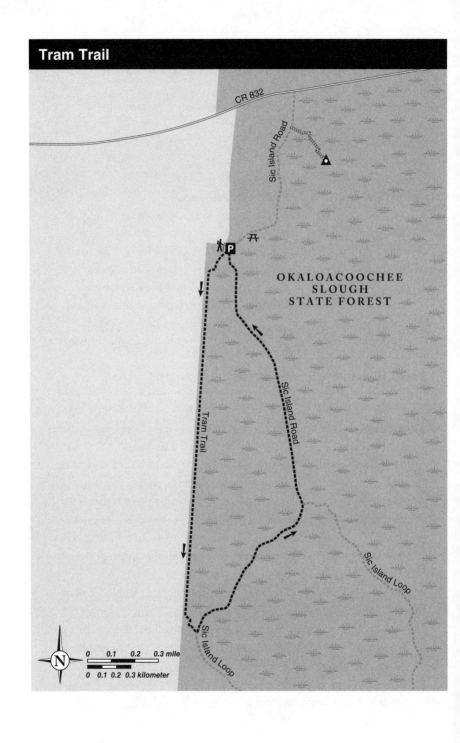

Tram Trail

CR 832

Sic Island Road

OKALOACOOCHEE
SLOUGH
STATE FOREST

Tram Trail

Sic Island Road

Sic Island Loop

Sic Island Loop

0   0.1   0.2   0.3 mile

0   0.1 0.2 0.3 kilometer

N

This tram cuts through otherwise wet woods.

were often called trams. In Florida, these trams were built up above the seasonally inundated forests that were timbered. A canal or ditch always parallels these trams, as the canals were a result of soil removal to build up the trams.

Turn left on the elevated, nearly arrow-straight southbound grade. Here in the Okaloacoochee Slough, land was wet more often than not. You will pass through pine areas, but it is mostly open grassy wetlands, willow thickets, or cypress domes. Along the canal, a watery ecosystem rises to drier plants. However, the sky is open overhead along the Tram Trail, necessitating sun protection.

While hiking the trail, try to imagine what the original Florida pioneers must have seen—wide open landscapes, much of it wet, all of it wild. There is hardly a way they could have kept their feet dry around the Okaloacoochee Slough. Of course, this elevated railroad grade, nearly a century old, makes our trip through the slough an easy one. You will also notice the great banks of clouds, hues of blue and white rising over the land. Okaloacoochee Slough is what I term Florida's "Big Sky Country," a land where low-slung swales and treeless terrain make for far-reaching panoramas that are more firmament than terra firma.

At 1.2 miles, a small wooden bridge spans a canal. At 1.6 miles, the Tram Trail leaves left from the old railroad grade. Dip from the grade and turn easterly. Reach Sic Island Road at 1.7 miles. Turn left here on the hard-packed, remote roadbed. Begin walking north amid mixed forest of palm, pine, and oak. Cardinals, robins, and other songbirds will urge you along. At 2.4 miles, the primitive Sic Island Loop, a four-wheel-drive road, leaves right. At 2.5 miles, the landscape opens to widespread vistas displaying multiple ecosystems at once—hardwood hammocks, cypress domes, pine thickets, and open wetlands. Soak in this unaltered parcel of the greater Everglades. At 3.0 miles, the forest closes in somewhat. Before you know it, the trailhead is just a few steps away. While you're here, try to incorporate dining into your hike at the shaded picnic area located near the trailhead.

Mileages at a Glance

0.0   Tram Trail trailhead
0.1   Join railroad grade
0.5   Loop turns back east
1.6   Left from railroad grade
1.7   North on Sic Island Road
3.5   Return to trailhead

16

Twin Mill Trail

Hike Summary: Enjoy solitude aplenty on this historic loop at Okaloacoochee Slough State Forest. Hike open terrain before entering a dark hardwood hammock. Come to Twin Mills, a former sawmill, and its giant sawdust pile. Continue through pines and grasses before closing the loop on Twin Mills Grade, a seldom-trod forest road presenting panoramic landscapes.

A giant sawdust pile left over from the logging days at Okaloacoochee Slough.

Distance: 2.4-mile loop
Hiking Time: 2.0 hours
Difficulty: Moderate
Highlights: Sawdust pile, hardwood hammock
Cautions: None
Fees/Permits: No fees or permits required
Best Seasons: November through April; check hunting dates
Other Trail Users: None. Leashed dogs allowed.
Trail Contacts: Okaloacoochee Slough State Forest, 6265 County Road 832, Felda, FL 33930, (863) 612-0776, www.floridaforestservice.com
Finding the Trailhead: From the intersection of FL 29 and FL 82, east of Fort Myers and north of Immokalee, take FL 29 north for 7.6 miles, then turn right onto Hendry County Road 832. Follow 832 east for 6.8 miles, passing the state forest building complex on your right. Turn left on Twin Mills Grade and follow it for 1.0 miles to reach the open grassy parking area on your left.
GPS Trailhead Coordinates: N26° 36.328', W81° 19.231'

Okaloacoochee Slough State Forest comes in at a whopping 32,000-plus acres. Located in Hendry County, between LaBelle and Immokalee, the reserve feeds water to both the Fakahatchee Strand and the Big Cypress Preserve downstream, recharging the Floridan Aquifer. This is strictly a winter-only hiking trail, as during the summer rainy season the path will be underwater in many places. Be apprised that fall weekends are popular hunting times at the forest, but the hunting season is generally over by December.

The rich slough forests and surrounding pinelands were first logged in the early 1900s. Railroads were spreading fast through South Florida, and railroad ties were needed in large number. The lumber extracted from Okaloacoochee Slough provided the timber for ties. The lumber was milled on-site using portable sawmills.

The hike leaves from Twin Mills Grade and enters a seasonal grassy wetland. The trail is marked with posts and blazes. Myrtles and pines rise from the grasses. The woods close in, and you

Twin Mill Trail

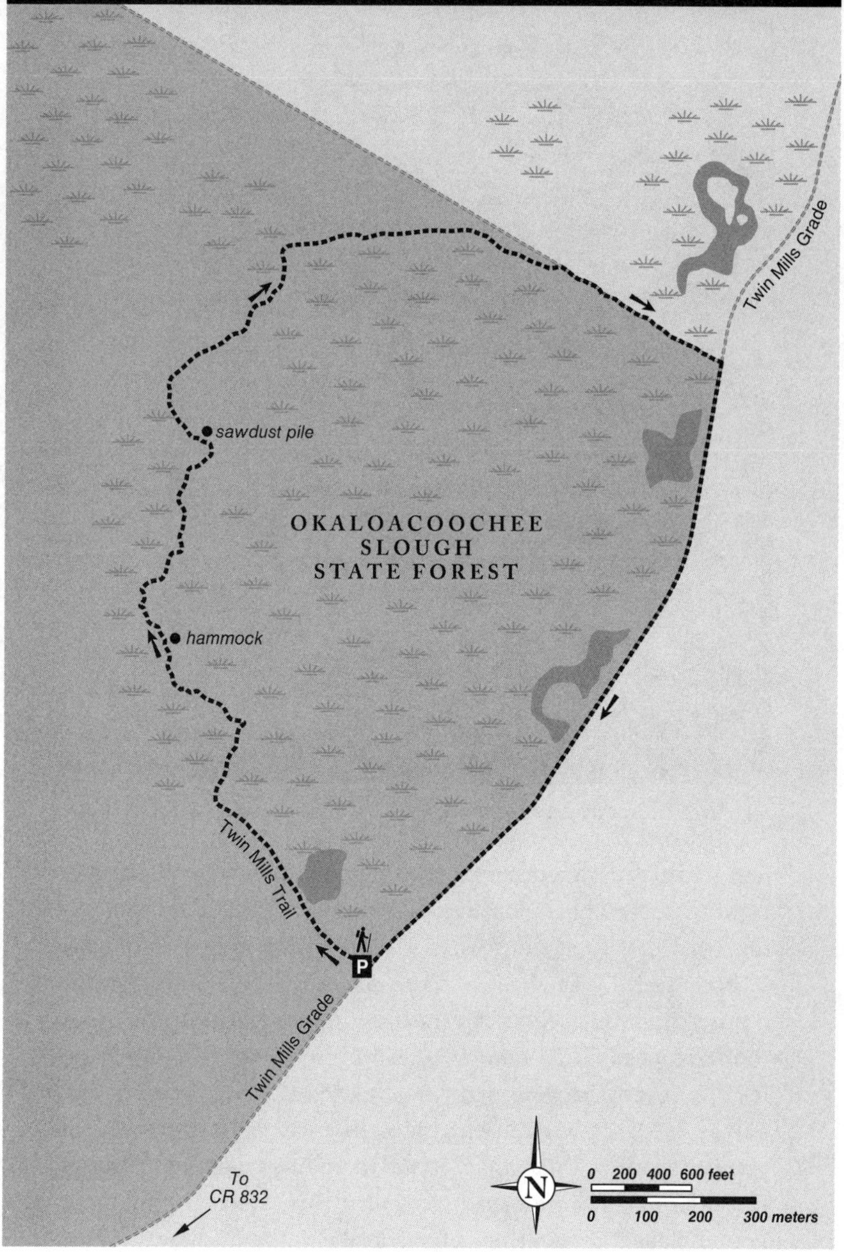

sawdust pile

OKALOACOOCHEE
SLOUGH
STATE FOREST

hammock

Twin Mills Trail

Twin Mills Grade

Twin Mills Grade

To
CR 832

N

0   200 400 600 feet

0   100   200   300 meters

A palm cathedral shades the path.

join a ditch-bordered berm. At .3 mile, the trail curves sharply right to enter a lush pine/live oak hammock, with the usual understory species such as white stopper, wild coffee, and ferns. Watch carefully at .4 mile as the trail turns left and becomes a pure singletrack footpath meandering underneath the hammock. Note the high canopy here. The palms are spaced just so, letting in very little sunlight, along with the outstretched live oak branches covered in epiphytes. The woods' roof fashions a green cathedral. Thick undergrowth combined with lesser use of this trail make the footbed somewhat dim. However, the path is well blazed, preventing getting lost. An open wetland can be seen through the trees to your right.

Leave the hammock and hike through a kaleidoscope of landscapes—pines, grassy openings, scrub oaks, palmetto. At .8 mile, reach the old sawdust pile. The elevated hill is hard to miss in this horizontal country. However, some vegetation has grown up on it, including small pine trees. Only until you start walking atop it do you realize that it truly is sawdust. The spongy texture and looseness gives it away. It's hard to imagine the pile being here for decades. In a flat area such as Okaloacoochee Slough, the elevation of the sawdust pile gives you a different perspective of the surrounding terrain. As you stand atop the sawdust pile, imagine how it was back then. The noise of the mill and men moving with purpose versus the whistling of the wind in the pines and the lack of humanity in what has become a backwater.

The Twin Mills Trail resumes its circuit through the evolving forest, more open than not, with low-slung palmetto, small oaks draped with Spanish moss, and small clearings. The trail curves east. Views of wetland swales open in the distance. Leave the footbed for a rough four-wheel-drive road at 1.4 miles. Keep cruising easterly to reach Twin Mills Grade at 1.6 miles. Here, turn right, southbound, on the hard-packed track. Despite its being called a road, Twin Mills Grade is seldom driven and provides easy walking. Landscapes of interior South Florida open without having to watch your every step. You will be traveling alongside a canal and will probably see alligators, turtles, and birds. Private land stretches across the canal and avails insight into what most of rural South Florida used to be—cattle country, home of the original cowboys, the Florida cracker. Watch for a small pond to the right of Twin Mills Grade just before reaching the trailhead at 2.4 miles.

Mileages at a Glance

- 0.0 Twin Mills trailhead
- 0.3 Enter hardwood hammock
- 0.8 Sawdust pile
- 1.6 Right on Twin Mills Grade
- 2.4 Return to trailhead

17

Indigo Trail at Ding Darling Refuge

Hike Summary: Enjoy a trek on this Sanibel Island national wild-life preserve. After touring the visitor center, begin a loop that first takes you along the woods and waters of Wildlife Drive, popular with hikers, bicyclers, and cars—and birdlife! Leave the drive and then take the Indigo Trail, a crushed-shell path through interior island woods, back to the visitor center.

Black-eyed Susans
color the refuge.

Distance: 4.1-mile loop

Hiking Time: 2.5 hours

Difficulty: Moderate

Highlights: Estuarine waters of Gulf Island

Cautions: Sun exposure

Fees/Permits: Entrance fee for Wildlife Drive required

Best Seasons: November through April; Wildlife Drive closed on Fridays

Other Trail Users: Autos and bikes on Wildlife Drive. Leashed dogs allowed.

Trail contacts: Ding Darling National Wildlife Refuge, 1 Wildlife Drive, Sanibel, FL 33957, (239) 472-1100, www.fws.gov/dingdarling/

Finding the Trailhead: From exit 131 on I-75 south of Fort Myers, take Daniels Parkway west for 4.6 miles, then turn left on Tamiami Trail, US 41 south, and follow it 1.2 miles to turn right on Gladiolus. Follow Gladiolus for 1.2 miles, then veer left on Summerlin Road and follow it for 6.2 miles to reach a traffic light. Keep straight here, now on Mc-Gregor Road. Follow McGregor Road for 5.3 miles to reach Periwin-kle Road. Turn right on Periwinkle and follow it for 2.4 miles to veer right onto Palm Ridge Road (it turns into Sanibel-Captiva Road). Follow Palm Ridge Road for 2.3 miles to the main refuge entrance on your right. Park at the refuge visitor center parking area.

GPS Trailhead Coordinates: N26° 26.731', W82° 6.780'

Originally named Sanibel Island National Wildlife Refuge, this 6,400-acre preserve harbors a variety of environments in which a greater variety of wildlife call home or use the refuge as a migratory stopover. In the first half of the 1900s, as America was spreading its wings and becoming more coastal-oriented, places such as Sanibel Island began to be developed as vacation getaways and the like. Conservation champions like as J. N. "Ding" Darling began crusading for areas that wildlife could call home. Darling, an avid hunter and fisherman, realized that if the birds and the beasts had no habitat, the wildlife would disappear, not only for hunters and anglers, but for the population at large. Darling's idea of a duck stamp for hunters began funding habitat

Indigo Trail at Ding Darling Refuge

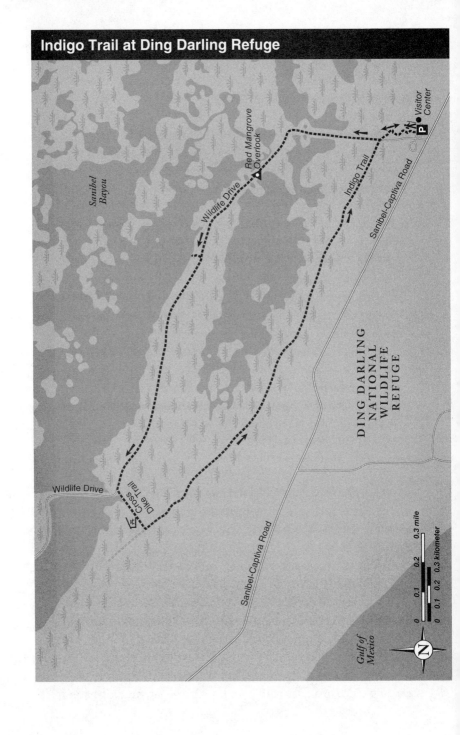

Wildflowers brighten even the pages of a hiking guide.

for waterfowl. To honor Darling, this Southwest Florida island refuge was renamed for him. Today, you can engage in multiple activities at the refuge, including hiking.

As you face the visitor center from the parking lot, look left for the Indigo Trail. The path leads under an elevated building and into gorgeous coastal maritime hammock forest of gumbo-limbo, sea grape, and sabal palm, before emerging at Wildlife Drive at .2 mile. From here, turn right onto Wildlife Drive. Just ahead you will see a manned kiosk where visitors pay a nomi-nal fee to walk Wildlife Drive. This trail is popular with hikers and bicyclists, so don't be deterred by the name. Instead, begin walking the wide paved track past mangrove-bordered brackish ponds that attract myriad birdlife. Alligator sightings are popu-lar with the snowbirds who flock to the refuge from up north. These tidally affected ponds churn back and forth under the bridges of the drive. The wetlands change with the rise and fall of the tides. You may see kayakers exploring the refuge by water. In other places, the waters will be obscured by dense vegetation.

At .5 mile, Wildlife Drive curves left, westerly. At 1.1 miles, reach the Red Mangrove Overlook. Here a spur trail leads through the saltwater evergreens onto a tree-lined pool. Look for birds feeding in this shallow estuary. Continue walking Wildlife Drive on a shoulder wide enough where the slow-moving vehicles are not a nuisance. At 1.9 miles, leave Wildlife Drive and come to the Cross Dike Trail. All cars are left behind. Restrooms and shaded shelters are situated here.

At 2.2 miles, reach the Indigo Trail. Ignore the user-created path going right here. Instead, turn left on a hard-packed crushed-shell track bordered by shallow mangrove canals and palms, strangler figs, and sea grapes on higher ground. This is the best part of the hike for trail conditions and visual remoteness. All too soon, at 3.9 miles, the Indigo Trail ends and you are back at Wildlife Drive. From this point, it is a .2 mile backtrack to the visitor center. While here, stop in and learn more about the refuge. Also, check for the array of guided treks that take place at Ding Darling.

Mileages at a Glance

0.0   Ding Darling Refuge Visitor Center
0.2   Right on Wildlife Drive
1.9   Left on Cross Dike Trail
2.2   Left on Indigo Trail
3.9   Return to Wildlife Drive
4.1   Return to trailhead

18

Sanibel-Captiva Nature Center

Hike Summary: This hike, on a tract managed by a private conservation foundation, explores the interior of Sanibel Island.
Wander through woodland to come alongside the Sanibel River.
Reach an observation tower and climb to extensive island views.
From there, loop through maritime hardwoods, highlighted
with interpretive information. Wetlands border the trail in
many places and present wildlife viewing opportunities.

A view of Sanibel Island from the observation tower.

Distance: 1.9-mile loop

Hiking Time: 1.5 hours

Difficulty: Easy

Highlights: Multiple environments, observation tower

Cautions: Lots of trail intersections

Fees/Permits: Entrance fee required

Best Seasons: November through April; trails open 8:30 a.m.–4 p.m.

Other Trail Users: None. No dogs allowed.

Trail Contacts: Sanibel-Captiva Conservation Foundation, 3333 Sanibel-Captiva Road, Sanibel, FL 33957, (239) 472-2329, www.sccf.org

Finding the Trailhead: From exit 131 on I-75 south of Fort Myers, take Daniels Parkway west for 4.6 miles, then turn left on Tamiami Trail, US 41 south, and follow it 1.2 miles to turn right on Gladiolus. Follow Gladiolus for 1.2 miles; then veer left on Summerlin Road and follow it for 6.2 miles to reach a traffic light. Keep straight here, now on McGregor Road. Follow McGregor Road for 5.3 miles to reach Periwinkle. Turn right on Periwinkle and follow it for 2.4 miles to veer right onto Palm Ridge Road (it turns into Sanibel-Captiva Road). Follow Sanibel-Captiva Road for 1.4 miles to reach the SCCF Nature Center on your left.

GPS Trailhead Coordinates: N26° 26.322', W82° 5.840'

In the 1960s, residents of Sanibel Island saw that the causeway connecting their island to the mainland, along with the increased availability of freshwater, would open the isle to development, perhaps to ruin the very thing that made Sanibel attractive in the first place—its natural beauty. By 1967, the Sanibel-Captiva Conservation Foundation was formed "to preserve natural resources and wildlife habitat on and around the islands of Sanibel and Captiva. They didn't want Southwest Florida and its islands to suffer the same fate as Miami and the metropolitan east coast of Florida. Since then, the foundation has worked to preserve the beauty of the islands in numerous ways, most visibly its acquisition of lands on Sanibel and Captiva. Today, the foundation owns nearly 2,000 acres, the centerpiece of which is the Center Tract, where this hike takes place.

Sanibel-Captiva Nature Center

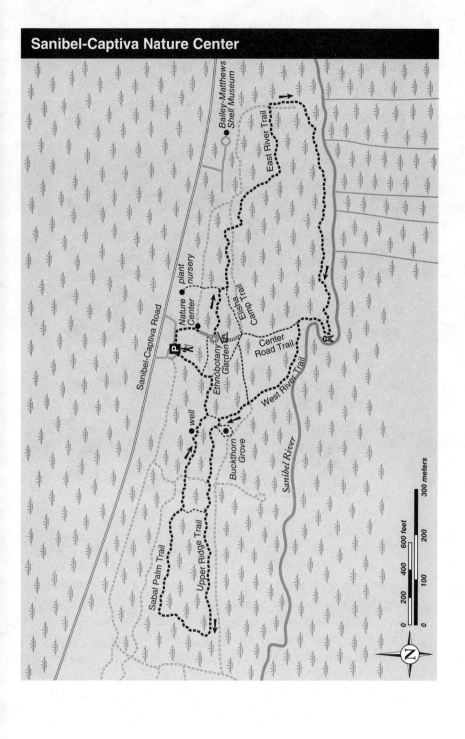

A leftover well from the pre-tourist days on Sanibel Island.

Located in the interior of Sanibel Island, the Center Tract harbors freshwater wetlands as well as uplands where maritime hardwoods grace the trailside terrain. Start your hike by entering the worth-a-visit nature center, then exiting the back onto an elevated boardwalk crossing a small marsh. Descend to the main trailhead to find an interesting ethnobotany garden, which details the use of plants by pre-Columbian residents of Sanibel Island. After exploring the garden, head left on the natural-surface East River Trail. Pass a trail to a plant nursery on your left and then the Elisha Camp Trail on your right. Break off from the maze of paths astride the nature center, hiking among palms, spartina grass, and ferns. Gumbo-limbos, buttonwoods, and maritime hardwoods form tree copses. At .4 mile, the trail joins an elevated berm. Cruise through junglelike wooded wetlands; roller-coaster over small spoil hills alongside the Sanibel River. Reach the park observation tower at .8 mile. Climb the wooded structure to see the forest and civilization of this Gulf island. Looking over the terrain makes you appreciate this preserve.

Head away from the tower on the Center Road Trail via boardwalk. At .9 mile, turn left on the West River Trail. Enjoy a little more walking along the Sanibel River before meeting the Elisha Camp Trail at 1.0 mile. Stay left here, still on the West River Trail. It morphs into a long boardwalk. At 1.1 miles, turn left toward Buckthorn Grove. The small loop circles through the dense Buckthorn Grove. Stay left, on the Upper Ridge Trail. Wander west in woods, crossing a couple of service roads. Make sure to look for the path with the hiker symbol here. At 1.2 miles, a shortcut leads right to the Sabal Palm Trail. Loop north to join the Sabal Palm Trail. The grassy track turns east and enters a gorgeous palm hammock, with hundreds of palms lining the trail. Their blackened trunks reveal fire being used to maintain the ecosystem.

Pass a couple of trail intersections, keeping east toward the nature center. Come to an old well at 1.7 miles. It is hard to believe the woodland around you was once farm fields a century back. At 1.8 miles, reenter the maze of nature trails near the nature center. Reach the Center Road Trail. Turn left here to emerge at the parking area at 1.9 miles.

Mileages at a Glance

0.0 SCCF Nature Center
0.8 Observation tower
1.1 Buckthorn Grove
1.7 Old well
1.9 Return to Nature Center parking area

19

Bailey Tract at Ding Darling Refuge

Hike Summary: This walk at the famed Sanibel Island wildlife refuge travels along open trails bordering a freshwater wetland, rare on the Gulf islands. You will first follow the now-channelized Sanibel River, an unusual freshwater stream in the interior island. Follow its turns; then reach ponds where waterfowl and other freshwater birds are seen in season. This loop is popular with locals for daily exercise.

Hiker soaks in the sunshine on the Bailey Tract.

Distance: 1.4-mile loop

Hiking Time: 1.0 hours

Difficulty: Easy

Highlights: Freshwater ponds

Cautions: Sun exposure

Fees/Permits: No fees or permits required

Best Seasons: Year-round

Other Trail Users: Bicyclists. Leashed dogs allowed.

Trail Contacts: Ding Darling National Wildlife Refuge, 1 Wildlife Drive, Sanibel, FL 33957, (239) 472-1100, www.fws.gov/dingdarling/

Finding the Trailhead: From exit 131 on I-75 south of Fort Myers, take Daniels Parkway west for 4.6 miles, then turn left on Tamiami Trail, US 41 south, and follow it 1.2 miles to turn right on Gladiolus. Follow Gladiolus for 1.2 miles, then veer left on Summerlin Road and follow it for 6.2 miles to reach a traffic light. Keep straight here, now on McGregor Road. Follow McGregor Road for 5.3 miles to reach Periwinkle Road. Turn right on Periwinkle Road and follow it 2.7 miles to Tarpon Bay Road. Turn left on Tarpon Bay Road. Follow it .5 mile to the right turn into the Bailey Tract parking area.

GPS Trailhead Coordinates: N26° 25.717′, W82° 4.839′

A narrow barrier island such as Sanibel has limited freshwater environments. And an island as developed as Sanibel has even fewer freshwater environments through which you can hike. Fortunately, the Bailey Tract is a 100-acre holding managed by the Ding Darling National Wildlife Refuge. It was originally owned by Frank Bailey, an islander whose family still lives and conducts business on Sanibel.

When the parcel was originally obtained by the Fish and Wildlife Service, they constructed dikes, ponds, and canals to attract waterfowl. Although the parcel was altered to favor wildlife, long-term plans are to restore this to marsh habitat. For now, however, we have the dikes for walking and the aquatic habitats for observing birds.

This hike loops around the outermost trail of the tract, the Red Trail. If you want to extend your hike, it is a simple matter of

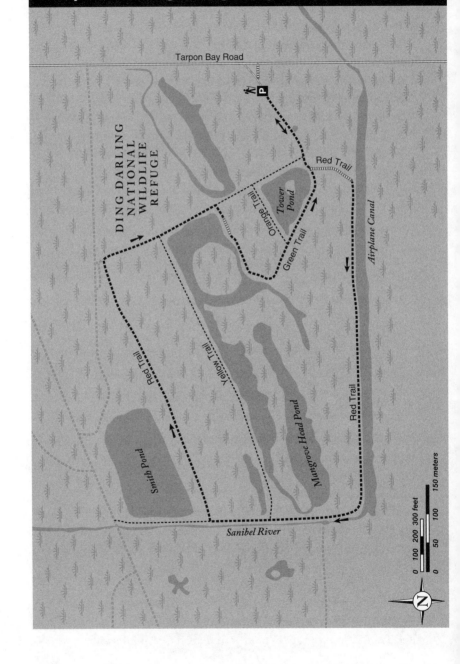

Bailey Tract at Ding Darling Refuge

Tarpon Bay Road

P

DING DARLING
NATIONAL
WILDLIFE
REFUGE

Red Trail

Tower Pond

Orange Trail

Green Trail

Airplane Canal

Red Trail

Yellow Trail

Red Trail

Smith Pond

Mangrove Head Pond

Sanibel River

0 100 200 300 feet

0 50 100 150 meters

N

A bat house on the Bailey Tract functions as a natural mosquito reducer.

picking up other dike trails traversing the Bailey Tract. Leave the parking area and soon come to a kiosk near the Tower Pond. Turn left here, joining the Red Trail. It travels a boardwalk to reach the Airplane Canal. The name comes from the canal—along which you are walking—being used as a takeoff/landing locale by the refuge's first manager, Tommy Wood, for his wildlife surveys of the island and refuge. You likely won't observe seaplanes in the canal, but you may see alligators and turtles basking in the sun along the bank of the Airplane Canal.

The trail is open to the sun overhead but bordered by palms. At .5 mile, the Red Trail abruptly turns right, north, still cruising a canal that was originally the Sanibel River. Gain glimpses of the Mangrove Head Pond to your right, while cruising along the freshwater Sanibel River to your left. At .6 mile, the Yellow Trail leaves right to shortcut the loop. Stay straight on the Red Trail. At .7 mile, the Red Trail turns right, and heads northeast. A service road keeps straight for Island Inn Road.

The walking is easy. You will see exercise-oriented hikers determinedly walking while wildlife-watchers will be taking their time. Note the bat houses set up for natural mosquito control. Strangler figs, buttonwoods, and sea grapes border the trail. Strangler figs are a fascinating tree. The large, fast-growing tree, native to South Florida, extends north into the central state and south to the Keys. What separates the strangler fig from other trees is how it begins life. It is a parasite. Strangler fig seeds lodge in crevices of other trees, such as palms, then send roots downward. These roots eventually reach the ground, forming their own underground root system, while continuing to grow around its host tree, often overwhelming and "strangling" the host. Strangler figs, also called banyan trees, can grow 60 feet high and reach 4 feet across at the trunk.

At 1.0 mile, the trail heads south, and passes the Yellow Trail coming in on the right. Come back along Mangrove Head Pond. Here, you may see the three major bird types from waterfowl such as ducks, to raptors such as osprey, and even wading birds like ibises and herons. At 1.1 miles, turn right onto the Green Trail, circling more open water. The Green Trail leads toward the Tower Pond. Pass the Orange Trail, a short path that circles Tower Pond, returning to the trail kiosk at 1.4 miles. From here it is but a short backtrack to the trailhead.

Mileages at a Glance

    0.0 Parking area off Tarpon Bay Road
    0.5 Red Trail turns right, north
    0.7 Red Trail turns right, northeast
    1.0 Red Trail turns right, south
    1.1 Right onto Green Trail
    1.4 Return to trailhead

20

Matanzas Pass Preserve

Hike Summary: Hike one of the last remaining native plant communities on Estero Island. The 60-acre tract contains two interconnected loops of both boardwalk and natural-surface trails. First, you will wander through mangrove forest, opening onto Estero Bay. The loop turns inland and makes its way to the next loop, a mix of maritime hardwood hammock forest and salt-influenced vegetation. Enjoy this interplay of fresh and salt environments before returning to the trailhead.

Mangrove frames the view of Estero Bay.

Distance: 1.4-mile loop

Hiking Time: 1.5 hours

Difficulty: Easy

Highlights: Island maritime hammock forest, views of Estero Bay

Cautions: None

Fees/Permits: No fees or permits required

Best Seasons: Year-round

Other Trail Users: None. No dogs allowed.

Trail Contacts: Lee County Parks & Recreation, 199 Bay Rd., Fort Myers Beach, FL 33931, (239) 533-7444, www.leeparks.org

Finding the Trailhead: From exit 131 on I-75 south of Fort Myers, take Daniels Parkway, Lee County Road 876, west to US 41, Tamiami Trail. Turn left on US 41 and follow it 1.2 miles to Gladiolus. Turn right on Gladiolus and follow it 1.1 miles to veer left on Summerlin Road, Lee County Road 869. Follow Summerlin Road for 3.5 miles to Lee County Road 865, head south on 865 toward Fort Myers Beach, and cross onto Estero Island. Stay with 865, Estero Boulevard, for 4.2 miles to turn left on Bay Road. Follow Bay Road a short distance to reach the preserve. It has a small parking area; you might have park on Estero Boulevard. *Alternate directions:* From exit 111 on I-75 north of Naples, take Bonita Beach Road west a total of 16.7 miles to reach Bay Road. Along the way you will bridge islands, reaching Estero Island. Turn right on Bay Road and follow it a short distance to dead-end at the trailhead.

GPS Trailhead Coordinates: N26° 26.9627', W81° 56.2766'

Southwest Florida has been viewed as an alluring beach escape for many a decade. Estero Island proves such. Ever since the 1940s, the island just off the coast near Fort Myers has been a beach destination. It started with small cottages and expanded to condos, hotels, and more. It remains a very popular vacation destination for visitors from afar, as well as day visitors from nearby towns. As the island evolved, the natural aspects of the landscape were altered until there was very little native habitat left. Matanzas Pass Preserve came to be as a result of this realization. Now the 60 acres keep intact a slice of Estero Island in

Matanzas Pass Preserve

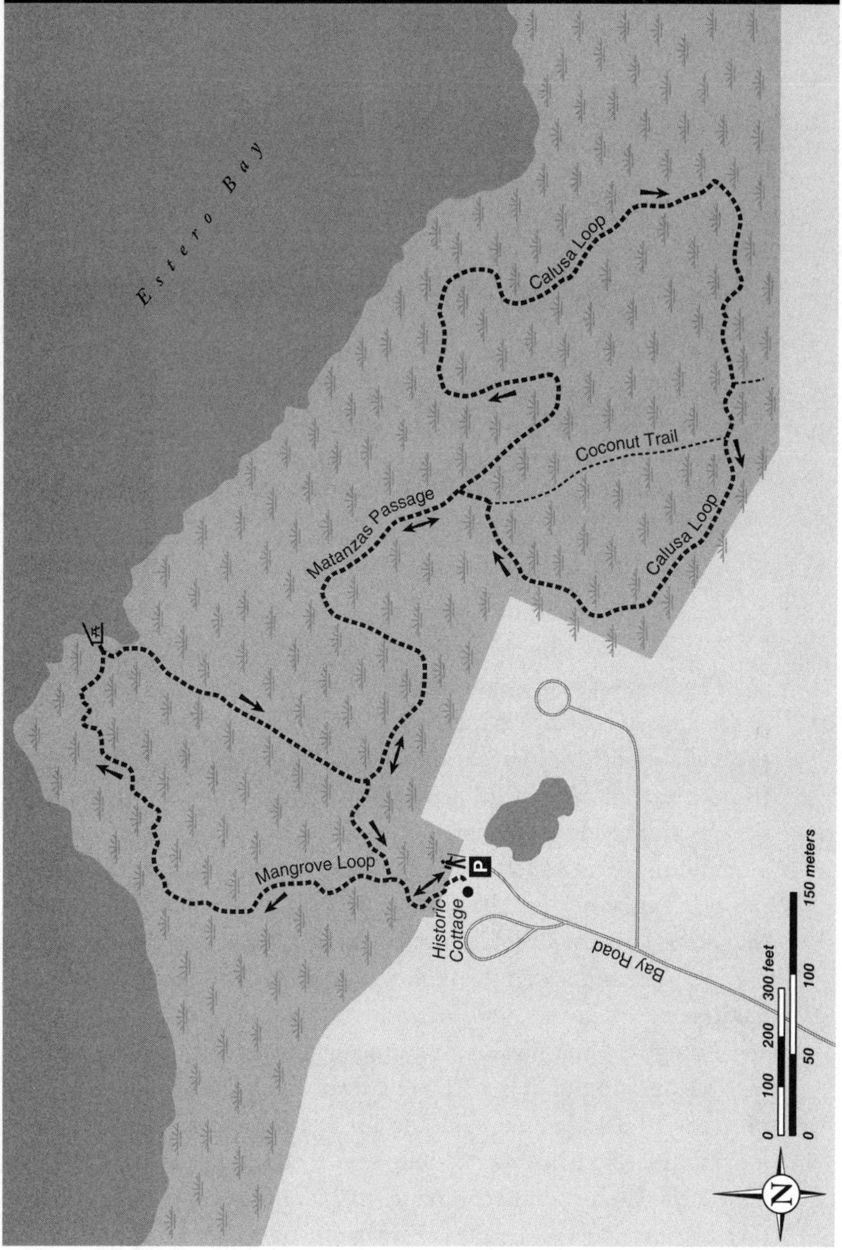

Estero Bay

Calusa Loop

Coconut Trail

Calusa Loop

Matanzas Passage

Mangrove Loop

Historic Cottage

P

Bay Road

0 100 200 300 feet
0 50 100 150 meters

N

A water barrel from an historic cottage at the trailhead.

its natural state, in addition to preserving a historic cottage that harkens back to a time when Southwest Florida and its gorgeous coastline was a sleepy, forgotten place.

The historic cottage is intermittently open for visitation. See the park website for hours and dates. Interestingly, you can view the last remaining water barrel from Estero Island. In the old days, island residents gathered their water from rain runoff and stored it in barrels, such as the one next to the historic cottage. Begin the hike next to the cottage, immediately coming to the Mangrove Loop. Head left, entering the last remaining maritime hardwood hammock on the island. Sea grape, cat's claw, and live oak rise on higher ground, while mangrove occupies lower areas. Soon join a boardwalk wandering in mangrove, interspersed with higher ground of maritime hardwoods. After .3 mile, open onto Estero Bay. A spur trail leads left to a covered shelter overlooking the estuarine waters. Step over a little tidal creek, passing a kayak landing, and complete the Mangrove Loop. Stay left on a boardwalk, the Matanzas Passage, wandering through buttonwood and mangrove mixed with a few hardy ferns. This area was once full of exotics, but the site was restored after becoming managed by Lee County.

At .6 mile, reach the Calusa Loop. Stay left here, joining another boardwalk, burrowing through mangrove, although the slightest elevation changes take you back to maritime hammock. Come very near Estero Bay. Curve back toward the island interior. Come close to habitations but stay with the trail, passing through a restored maritime forest to meet the Coconut Trail at 1.0 mile. Stay straight, continuing the longer Calusa Loop and soon meet the Coconut Trail again at 1.3 miles. Stay left here and then backtrack to the trailhead, completing your hike.

Mileages at a Glance

0.0 Matanzas Pass Preserve trailhead
0.3 Estero Bay Pavilion
0.6 Left on Calusa Loop
1.0 Coconut Trail
1.4 Return to trailhead

21

Estero Bay Preserve Hike

Hike Summary: Take a walk on the strange side at Winkler Point. Traverse a transitional zone between wooded uplands and Estero Bay. Barren salt flats, tidal marsh, mangrove patches, and evolving terrain reclaimed from exotic vegetation make a unique hiking palette to explore. Start in pines, palms, and palmetto flatwoods and then turn toward bleak salt flats. The hike then visits a tidal pond ringed in mangrove before turning past more salt flats. Finally, return to pines before completing the hike.

Salt flats are a barren but essential part of Southwest Florida's coastal ecosystem.

Distance: 2.5-mile loop

Hiking Time: 1.5 hours

Difficulty: Moderate

Highlights: Salt flats, mangrove woods

Cautions: Avoid unmarked side trails

Fees/Permits: No fees or permits required

Best Seasons: November through April

Other Trail Users: None. Leashed dogs allowed.

Trail contacts: Estero Bay Preserve State Park, 3300 Corkscrew Road, Estero, FL 33928, (239) 992-0311, www.floridastateparks.com

Finding the Trailhead: From exit 131 on I-75 south of Fort Myers, take Daniels Parkway, Lee County Road 876 west, to US 41, Tamiami Trail. Turn left on US 41 and follow it 1.2 miles to Gladiolus. Turn right on Gladiolus and follow it 1.1 miles to veer left on Summerlin Road, Lee County 869. Follow Summerlin Road for .8 mile to Winkler Road. Turn left on Winkler Road and follow it 2.3 miles to dead-end at the trailhead.

GPS Trailhead Coordinates: N26° 28.819', W81° 53.906'

Bring a hat and sunscreen, as the entire trek is open to the sky above. The trails start east of the parking area. The preserve uses a system of color-coded trails to make interconnected loops. Walk through a small gate and then reach a kiosk and the preserve. Stay left, heading easterly along the preserve boundary on the Orange Trail, on a firebreak bordered by scrub pines, palmettos, and oaks. You'll also likely see standing dead trunks of melaleuca trees, relics of the ongoing battle between exotic and native Florida vegetation. The Florida Park Service is continuing to remove exotics, but they persistently return, and the war seems endless, especially considering South Florida's long growing season. Pesticide spraying and prescribed fire are the two most common exotic-removal tactics.

At .2 mile, stay straight, joining the Yellow Trail. Here the Orange Trail turns right toward a seasonal pond. Keep along the preserve boundary. From the border you can see one of the problems with removing exotics: because adjacent private properties

Estero Bay Preserve Hike

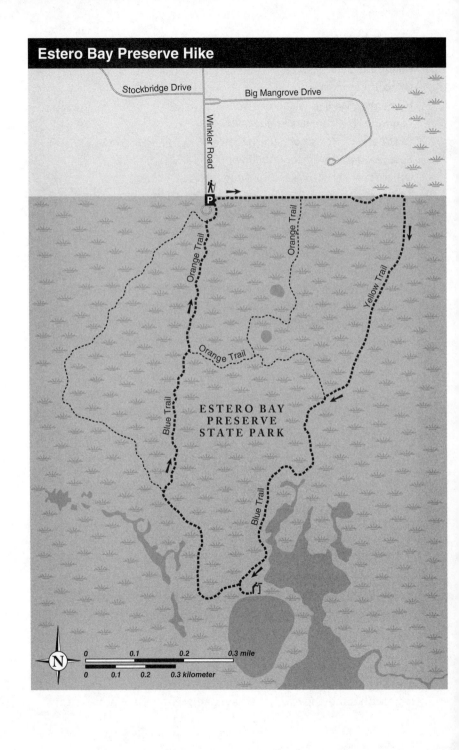

Stockbridge Drive

Big Mangrove Drive

Winkler Road

Orange Trail

Orange Trail

Yellow Trail

Orange Trail

Blue Trail

ESTERO BAY
PRESERVE
STATE PARK

Blue Trail

N

| 0 | 0.1 | 0.2 | 0.3 mile |

| 0 | 0.1 | 0.2 | 0.3 kilometer |

Strange pneumatophores add to an already strange landscape.

do not have to remove their non-native trees, the Brazilian pepper and melaleuca keep spilling into preserve. At .4 mile, the Orange Trail turns south to enter a plain pocked with a few scraggly mangroves. This forbidding landscape is your first taste of the salt flats that characterize much of the preserve. When storm events and high tides bring salt water over this saucer-like plain, it leaves very poor, salt-inundated soils in which few plants can grow. But the salt flats are every bit as much the natural Southwest Florida landscape as is a lush cypress swamp, albeit harder to appreciate. The salt flat does open views of the natural preserve in the fore and high-rises in the yon. At .9 mile, reach another intersection. Stay south, straight, joining the Blue Trail, as the Yellow Trail leaves right. Continue in the oddly remote preserve sandwiched between densely populated Estero Island to the west and the busy mainland to the east. Watch for deer and hog prints in the wet areas. Red-winged blackbirds bring a constant chatter.

Continue drifting through lightly wooded areas along with salt flats. Watch for unofficial spur trails made by hikers exploring the open flats. The official trails are marked with color-coded posts. During the dry season, the flats will be just that; in the rainy season, however, the trail system and surrounding terrain can be quite mucky. It is the natural order of things, though not a hiker-friendly situation. Black mangroves will grow in dense thickets bordering the salt flats. Watch for their strange, finger-like roots, known as pneumatophores, rising from the ground.

At 1.4 miles, a spur trail leads left to an observation deck overlooking a red mangrove-ringed lake. This is a potential birding destination. The main path loops back north, meeting the Orange Trail at 2.1 miles. Rejoin the Orange Trail heading into drier palmettos and pines. All too soon you are back at the trailhead, having visited this peculiar but natural phenomenon of coastal Southwest Florida.

Mileages at a Glance

0.0 Winkler Point trailhead
0.2 Orange Trail leaves right
0.4 Yellow Trail turns south
0.9 Stay south with the Blue Trail
1.4 Spur leads left to an observation deck
2.1 Rejoin Orange Trail, rise to uplands
2.5 Return to trailhead

22

Koreshan State Historic Site Hike

Hike Summary: Explore one of the most fascinating historic locales in Southwest Florida, set on the banks of the Estero River. Leave an attractive boat ramp and picnic area and then walk the deeply wooded shores of the Estero, where huge stands of bamboo stretch for the sky. Reach the preserved site of the Koreshan Unity Settlement, a strange sect led by one Cyrus Teed. Wander among many a preserved building and soak in the interpretive information of a fascinating Southwest Florida story. The balance of the hike parallels the park boundary among pines and grasses before returning to the trailhead.

One of the many authentic period buildings gracing Koreshan State Historic Site.

Distance: 1.8-mile loop
Hiking Time: 3.5 hours, including tour of Koreshan settlement
Difficulty: Easy
Highlights: Estero River, Koreshan settlement
Cautions: None
Fees/Permits: Entrance fee required
Best Seasons: November through April
Other Trail Users: None. Leashed dogs allowed.
Trail Contacts: Koreshan State Historic Site, 3800 Corkscrew Road, Estero, FL 33928, (239) 992-0311, www.floridastateparks.org
Finding the Trailhead: From exit 123 on I-75, head west on Corkscrew Road for 2 miles to a traffic light and US 41. Keep forward a short distance; then turn right into Koreshan State Historic Site. Stay straight beyond the ranger station; then veer left at .1 mile toward the boat ramp. Upon reaching the boat ramp, turn right into a parking loop. The hike starts in the northeast corner of the loop.
GPS Trailhead Coordinates: N26° 26.199', W81° 49.132'

Dr. Cyrus Teed, who renamed himself Koresh after an "illumination," founded a new version of Christianity based on communal living, celibacy, a universe inside the earth, and him being immortal. The part about the universe inside the earth was called "Cellular Cosmogony," which Koresh "discovered" in 1870. Enough people believed him and followed him to the remote Estero River in 1894 to form a community where they practiced what Teed preached. Each member of the sect was to work for the good of all. Both traditional and vocational educations were stressed, as was Koreshan Cosmogony and the how the world worked according to Koresh.

Then Teed died. After his lack of immortality was exposed, the sect began to dwindle until 1961, when remaining members donated the communal land to the state in Teed's memory. Thus, Koreshan State Historic Site was born.

Teed's followers were the first of what was to become "New Jerusalem," a planned city of millions. What you will see on the hike, the Home Grounds, was about as big as it got. Southwest

Koreshan State Historic Site Hike

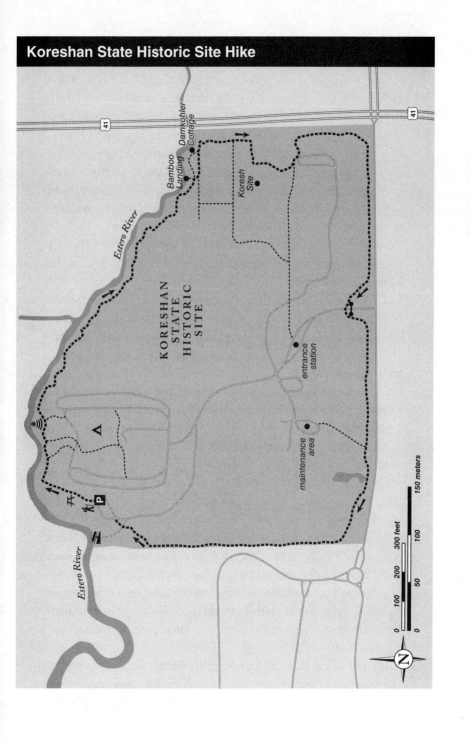

Florida, however, has grown to Teed's desired size. The hike begins at the park picnic area. Join a path passing through the shaded picnic grounds with a restroom. On the far side of the picnic area, pick up a sandy path running east along the Estero River. A sign will say, "Nature Trail." The tidally influenced Estero flows beside mangroves and under overhanging live oaks. Shortly pass an observation deck on your left, and several spur trails to the park campground. Pass around the campground amphitheater and stay left, traveling under Spanish moss–draped live oaks, and palms. Ahead, wild bamboo rises 30 or more feet in the air with trunks as thick as your arm!

At .5 mile, emerge onto the gardens and grounds of the Koreshan settlement. Explore at will. Bamboo Landing, part of the Koreshan settlement, is an Estero River boater-access point. The word "Estero" is Spanish for "estuary." The lush streamside environment is deserving of the name. The settlement gardens demonstrate the importance of form and order to the sect. The machine shop and bakery show the practical side of the Koreshans, who wanted to make life on the home ground both efficient and profitable. The Art Hall was the cultural and religious center of Koreshan life. View the stage, the paintings, and other relics of a doomed religion.

To continue the hike, keep south from the Art Hall, passing near the parking area for the historic district. The mileages described below do not count walking around the Koreshan historic site grounds. Come along busy US 41, then curve west along the quiet portion of Corkscrew Road tracing the park boundary. Curve away from the boundary and cross the park entrance road at 1.2 miles, right at the park gate. Continue cruising west on a grassy track amid scattered pines, returning to the boundary. You will see buildings of the park maintenance area to your right. At 1.4 miles, a spur leads right to the maintenance area. Stay straight, bridging a culvert, and then pass a pond to your right.

At 1.5 miles, the trail turns right, north, along the edge of the park. To your right are the native Florida forests and to your left, across the park boundary, a housing tract. That is Southwest

Florida in the twenty-first century. At 1.7 miles, keep straight as a fire road goes left along the expanded park boundary. Shortly, the boat-ramp parking area comes into view on your right, and a spur leads to it, taking you back to the point of origin.

Mileages at a Glance

- 0.0 Picnic area near the park boat ramp
- 0.5 Reach the grounds of the Koreshan Unity Settlement
- 1.2 Cross the park entrance road
- 1.4 Meet a spur to the park maintenance area; then pass a pond
- 1.5 Right at state park boundary, northbound
- 1.7 Stay straight as a fire road leads left
- 1.8 Emerge at boat-ramp parking area

23

CREW Marsh Hike

Hike Summary: This hike explores a host of Southwest Florida environments—pine flatwoods, seasonal marshes, tropical hardwood hammocks, and wooded sloughs in a large, wildlife-rich habitat. Your loop, on well-marked paths, leads to an observation deck alongside a seasonal pond before coming to a high tower overlooking the large wildland. Soak in panoramic views before crossing a dark cypress slough. The rich forest continues as you enter a live oak hammock. Reemerge into pines, completing the circuit.

A viewing tower provides panoramic views of CREW Marsh wetlands.

Distance: 3.0-mile loop
Hiking Time: 2.0 hours
Difficulty: Moderate
Highlights: Multiple ecosystems, observation tower
Cautions: None
Fees/Permits: No fees or permits required
Best Seasons: November through April
Other Trail Users: None. Leashed dogs allowed.
Trail Contacts: CREW Land & Water Trust, 23998 Corkscrew Road, Estero, FL 33928, (239) 657-2253, www.crewtrust.org
Finding the Trailhead: From exit 123 on I-75, travel 22 miles east on Corkscrew Rd. You will pass the CREW Cypress Dome Trails 3.4 miles before reaching the CREW Marsh trails, on your right.
GPS Trailhead Coordinates: N26° 29.510', W81° 32.031'

The CREW Land and Water Trust is a watershed-protection and aquifer-recharge area that protects the surface lands upon which hiking trails are laid. CREW stands for Corkscrew Regional Ecosystem Watershed. The greater CREW watershed, which flows through Corkscrew Swamp, comprises 60,000 acres in Lee and Collier Counties. The CREW Marsh area covers 5,000 acres. During the wet season, the CREW Marsh soaks in precipitation, filtering water before it descends into the Floridan Aquifer, porous rock strata below the land surface holding Southwest Florida's drinking water. Recharge zones such as the CREW Marsh not only keep the drinking water coming to your tap but also provide habitat for the plants and animals that call the area home. This includes the largest of local beasts—the black bear, as well as the elusive Florida panther. Your most likely wildlife sightings will be white-tailed deer or wild hogs.

The trailhead offers shaded picnic tables, an informative kiosk, and portable restroom. Leave the fenced trailhead on a wide, grassy track. Walk beneath tall pines to reach a split in the trail. Head left toward the observation deck on the Pine Flatwoods Trail. Soon reach a grassy pond and observation deck, likely to be dry during the cooler, drier hiking season. Continue looping

CREW Marsh Hike

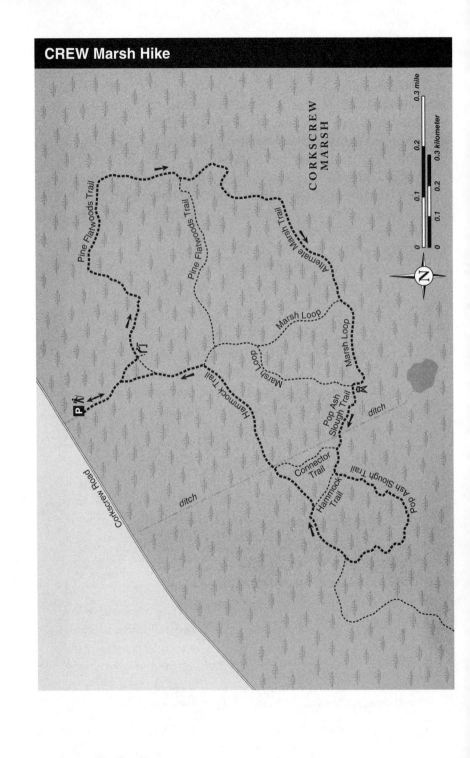

CORKSCREW MARSH

Corkscrew Road

Pine Flatwoods Trail

Pine Flatwoods Trail

Alternate Marsh Trail

Marsh Loop

Marsh Loop

Marsh Loop

Pop Ash Slough Trail

Hammock Trail

Connector Trail

Hammock Trail

Pop Ash Slough Trail

ditch

ditch

N

0   0.1   0.2   0.3 mile

0   0.1   0.2   0.3 kilometer

Entering verdant Pop Ash Slough.

through evergreens. Occasional service roads are marked as such, minimizing directional confusion. Bisect a live oak dome at .3 mile. Live oaks range throughout the Sunshine State. They favor sandy soils near marshes, not too wet but not too dry. Their wood burns hot and relatively smokeless. Live oaks were the reason for establishing Florida's first preserved forest. Back in 1828, President John Quincy Adams authorized the purchase of an extraordinary live oak stand in the Panhandle for shipbuilding purposes. The U.S. Navy needed the long and large curved woods of the live oak, ideal for building the ships of the day. The evolution of ironclad ships diminished the need for wooden vessels, but the property remained in government hands until becoming part of Gulf Islands National Seashore. Live oaks range from the Virginia coast to Florida, then west along the Gulf into Texas. Spanish moss–draped live oaks recall the slow, relaxed pace of the now-forgotten Old South.

The scenery continues changing from willowy wetlands to grassy marsh to oak cathedrals. At .8 mile, stay left with the Alternate Marsh Trail. Hike alongside open wetlands to your left and pine flatwoods to your right, a meeting of ecotones. Enriching views can be had across the wetlands. At 1.3 miles, reach the

Trekking through the wildlands of Southwest Florida.

Marsh Loop Trail. Stay left here, keeping the open marsh to your left.

Come to the large wooden observation tower at 1.5 miles. Gain commanding views of the distant marsh from atop the open tower. These open wetlands act as giant sponges when the thunderstorms of summer and fall rain down on Southwest Florida. Willow thickets, oak hammocks, and cypress domes occupy the distance, a natural mosaic of Southwest Florida.

Continue past the tower. Leave the Marsh Loop just ahead. Turn left onto the Pop Ash Slough Trail. Enjoy deciduous maple trees from a boardwalk as they change with the seasons. Cross an old ditch; then pass a connector trail leading right. Keep on the Pop Ash Slough Trail to meet the Hammock Trail at 1.7 miles. Stay left with the Pop Ash Slough Trail. Dense, fern-floored forest crowds the path. Join a boardwalk at 1.9 miles, passing through many a pop ash, a deciduous swamp tree. Walk through moss-covered trees in shade-cooled woods. Emerge from the hammock, and at 2.1 miles, a spur trail leads left to a primitive backcountry campsite. To use this campsite you must register ahead of time via the CREW website.

At 2.3 miles, the Hammock Trail enters on your right. Stay straight, soon reaching the Connector Trail and the ditch that funnels water into the marsh. The hike crosses the ditch and then wanders through pine flatwoods. At 2.7 miles, turn left onto the Marsh Trail, aiming for the trailhead. Soon you are backtracking to the trailhead and completing the hike.

Mileages at a Glance

0.0 CREW Marsh trailhead
0.8 Stay left with the Alternate Marsh Trail
1.5 Observation tower
1.9 Join a boardwalk before entering hardwood hammock
2.1 Spur trail to primitive campsite
3.0 Return to trailhead

24

CREW Cypress Dome Hike

Hike Summary: Experience solitude on this scenic and varied loop in protected wildland. The hike explores multiple environments, from oak halls to pinelands. The highlight of the hike traverses a tropical hammock for a solid mile of junglelike intrigue before emerging from the property's southeast corner. Head west along a canal in woods before immersing in tall cypress domes. The final part of the walk traverses open lands.

Distance: 4.4-mile loop
Hiking Time: 2.5 hours
Difficulty: Moderate
Highlights: Extended hike through tropical hammock
Cautions: Numerous intersections
Fees/Permits: No fees or permits required
Best Seasons: November through April
Other Trail Users: None. Leashed dogs allowed.
Trail contacts: CREW Land & Water Trust, 23998 Corkscrew Road, Estero, FL 33928, (239) 657-2253, www.crewtrust.org
Finding the Trailhead: From exit 123 on I-75, travel 18.6 miles east on Corkscrew Road. The trailhead will be on your right.
GPS Trailhead Coordinates: N26° 27.387', W81° 33.730'

Concern for Southwest Florida's drinking water led to the acquisition of this land and the trails that we can hike. The Corkscrew Regional Ecosystem Watershed (CREW) was formed in 1989 as a public-private partnership centered in Lee and Collier Counties.

CREW Cypress Dome Hike

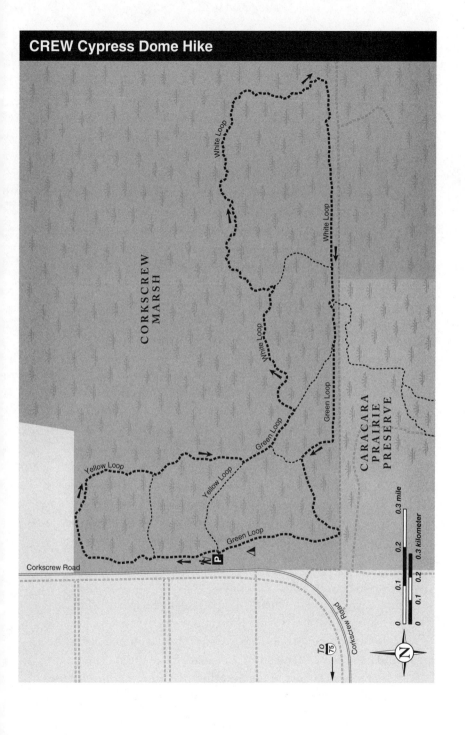

Its primary mission is to preserve the greater Corkscrew Swamp watershed, helping recharge the underground aquifer upon which Southwest Florida relies. It also protects the area from floods and provides fish and wildlife habitat and recreation areas for the citizenry, a winner all around.

CREW has acquired several tracts, and in conjunction with other preserves and mitigation areas, creates an aquifer recharge zone for the western Everglades. This particular hike takes place on what is known as the Cypress Dome Tract. Here, you can see firsthand wildlife habitats being preserved, as well as an example of slow recharge of the underground aquifer versus the fast run-off in urbanized areas. What is a wetland? According to the U.S. Environmental Protection Agency, wetlands are "lands where saturation with water is the dominant factor determining the nature of soil development and the types of plant and animal communities living in the soil and on its surface." Translation: a wetland is an ecosystem of which water is the key ingredient. One more part of the definition states, "Wetlands generally include swamps, marshes, bogs and similar areas." Therefore, wetlands can take varied forms.

The trail system is laid out in a system of color-coded trails with hiker symbols. Leave the parking area and look left for a wide path, the Yellow Loop. It heads north in a mix of scrub oaks, pines, palms, and palmettos. At .2 mile, a shortcut leaves right. Keep straight, only to turn south in live oaks. Reach the other end of the shortcut at .8 miles.

The Yellow Loop keeps southeast in pines to reach the Green Loop at 1.1 miles. Note the marsh at this intersection. Wetlands are scattered throughout the hike's perimeters, and are the "sponges" that absorb and filter rainwater and then slowly release the water into the aquifer below ground. The marsh is just one of the ever-changing habitats in this parcel. Stay left here, passing a shortcut leading right. By now you have noticed these wide hiking trails also act as firebreaks in managing the landscape here. At any given time, one side of the trail may have been recently burned while the other side has not. Fire is an important component in maintaining Southwest Florida's natural ecosystems. The area's wildlife, from bears to birds, thrives best in lands vegetated with flora native to South Florida.

At 1.3 miles, turn left onto the White Loop. Hike easterly in pine flatwoods, surrounded by open wetlands visible through the trees. At 1.7 miles, the trail suddenly leaves sharply left from the wide track onto a singletrack footpath. A wide service road keeps forward here. Look for the white blazes leading left into the woods. Soon enter a lush hammock, rife with live oaks, ferns, wild coffee, bromeliads, and pop ash. This is not a place to hike during the rainy season, as the forest floor can be a little damp, even in winter. Enjoy the extended walk through this deep wood. Surprisingly, come to a picnic table at 2.5 miles. Continue your hike through the cathedral-like hammock.

At 2.7 miles, emerge into a pine-bordered clearing in the southeastern corner of the tract. Ignore the service roads and stay right here with the white blazes, now heading westerly. A canal lies to your left. Walk amid a mix of woods. Reach a trail intersection at 3.3 miles. Here, a trail leads left to the Carcara Prairie Preserve. Stay straight on the White Trail and, at 3.4 miles, reach another intersection. Here, the Green Loop angles right and also keeps straight. Keep straight on the Green Loop, keeping the canal to your left. Pines, palms, and scrub oaks partially shade the grassy track.

At 3.7 miles, the Green Loop turns right, passing through a live oak hammock as it squeezes between cypress domes. At 3.8 miles, a shortcut trail leaves right; stay forward, cruising the margin between oaks and pines. The last part of the hike turns north, passing a primitive campsite just before reaching the trailhead at 4.4 miles.

Mileages at a Glance

0.0 CREW Cypress Dome trailhead
1.1 Join the Green Loop
1.7 White Loop enters hammock
2.7 Head west along a canal
3.8 Pass between cypress domes
4.4 Return to trailhead

25

Caracara Prairie Preserve

Hike Summary: If you enjoy palms and prairies, this hike is for you. To access the Caracara Prairie Preserve, use the trails of the CREW Cypress Dome Preserve, a scenic tract in its own right. Walk scattered pinelands and meadow and then reach Caracara Prairie Preserve. Trace a gorgeous palm strand between prairies. Make a circuit in mostly woods, crossing several gates—cattle are run here on a lease. Take a different route when returning through the CREW Cypress Dome, surveying more of the wildscape.

Live oaks and palms shade the trail.

Distance: 5.0-mile loop

Hiking Time: 3.0 hours

Difficulty: Moderate

Highlights: Two wildland preserves in one hike

Cautions: Numerous intersections.

Fees/Permits: No fees or permits required

Best Seasons: November through April; check hunting dates

Other Trail Users: None. No dogs allowed.

Trail Contacts: CREW Land & Water Trust, 23998 Corkscrew Road, Estero, FL 33928, (239) 657-2253, www.crewtrust.org

Finding the Trailhead: From exit 123 on I-75, travel 18.6 miles east on Corkscrew Road. The CREW Cypress Dome trailhead will be on your right.

GPS Trailhead Coordinates: N26° 27.387', W81° 33.730'

Though the preserve is named for a threatened buzzard, the most important function of these CREW lands is to help recharge the underground aquifer for Southwest Florida's burgeoning population. This preserve, with its many prairies, is ideal habitat for the crested caracara, for the bird—resembling a cross between a common vulture and an eagle—favors open habitat and even will share carrion with common buzzards. It is more common in Central America and South America but is found in Texas and Arizona, along with Florida.

Take note that both preserves are open to hunting so apprise yourself of forthcoming hunt dates via the above-listed website before you attempt a hike.

Leave the CREW Cypress Dome parking area via gate. Facing east, away from Corkscrew Road, three trails diverge. Head right, southbound on the Green Trail. The paths are marked with color-coded posts. Join a doubletrack sand road bordered with pines and palms. Quickly pass the preserve's primitive campsite, open by reservation only, on your left. It borders a large field.

Walk along the property edge; then, at .4 mile, veer left, easterly in thicker woods. A shallow canal runs to your right. Cruise a grassy path. The Caracara Prairie Preserve is just south, across

Caracara Prairie Preserve

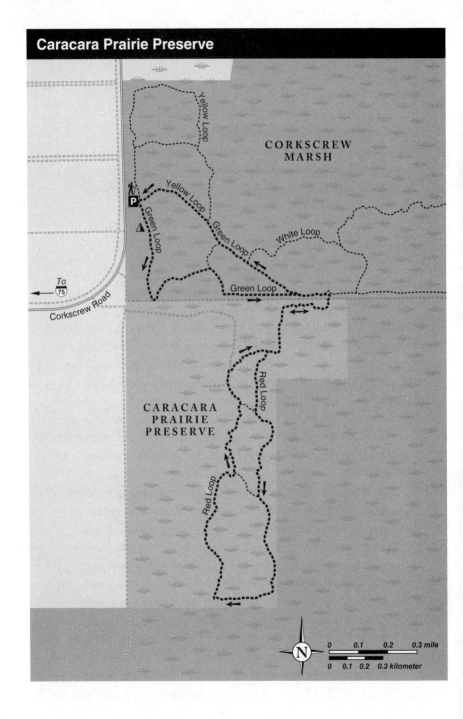

CORKSCREW MARSH

Yellow Loop

Yellow Loop

Green Loop

Green Loop

Green Loop

White Loop

Green Loop

P

To 75

Corkscrew Road

CARACARA PRAIRIE PRESERVE

Red Loop

Red Loop

Red Loop

N

| 0 | 0.1 | 0.2 | 0.3 mile |

| 0 | 0.1 | 0.2 | 0.3 kilometer |

Even the cows are wild at Caracara Prairie Preserve.

the canal. However, keep easterly, turning into a shady live oak hammock. Pass a blue-blazed shortcut path on your left at .6 mile. Rejoin the preserve boundary to reach a three-way trail intersection at 1.0 mile. Your return route, the Green Trail, cuts acutely left. You stay straight, now on the White Trail, bordered by laurel oaks and maple.

At 1.1 miles, come to another intersection. Turn right here, crossing the canal and a berm to reach the gated Caracara Prairie Preserve. Join the Red Trail as it turns west, snaking through mixed woods. At 1.3 miles, the Red Trail turns south. Join a palmy berm flanked by prairie on both sides. Work through a gate and then reach the loop portion of the Red Trail. Stay left and open onto a large meadow and wetland, dotted with bird-attracting ponds.

Meet a small palm strand and reach the blue shortcut #1 at 1.7 miles. Stay with the Red Trail in a mix of oak woods, palm stands, pines, and small clearings. Cattle will often be seen in the clearings. Intersect the blue shortcut #2 at 2.1 miles. The forest becomes denser with live oaks and pines. At 2.4 miles, the Red Trail turns westerly, confined by the preserve's boundaries, then turns north at 2.6 miles. Then comes what I believe is the most scenic part of the Caracara—a long palm strand overlooking prairies. Here, the path winds among linear palm cathedrals yet avails glances into the sun-burnished prairies beyond.

At 3.1 miles, intersect the other end of blue shortcut #2. Continue with the Red Trail. At 3.4 miles, pass blue shortcut #1, weaving among palms aplenty. Briefly join a gravel service road and then leave right, back into palms. Complete the loop portion of the Caracara Prairie Preserve Trail at 3.7 miles. From here, backtrack into the Crew Cypress Dome Preserve and meet the Green Trail at 4.2 miles. This time, leave right on the Green Trail, angling northwesterly in open pine woodland on a grassy track. At 4.4 miles, pass the White Trail on your right. Stay straight with the Green Trail, passing the Blue Trail on your left at 4.5 miles. Then, at 4.6 miles, meet the Yellow Trail. Stay straight as it aims for the trailhead in pines. Finally, reach the trailhead at 5.0 miles, returning to the CREW Cypress Dome parking area and the hike's end.

Mileages at a Glance

0.0 CREW Cypress Dome trailhead
1.0 Meet the White Trail
1.1 Right on the Red Loop, enter Caracara Prairie Preserve
1.3 Left on Red Trail at loop
1.7 Blue shortcut #1 leaves right
2.1 Blue shortcut #2 leaves right
2.6 Red Trail turns north
3.1 Blue shortcut #2 leaves right
3.4 Blue shortcut #1 leaves right
3.7 Complete Red Trail loop, backtrack to Green Trail
4.4 Right on Green Trail
4.6 Straight on Yellow Trail
5.0 Return to trailhead

Black Island Trail

Hike Summary: Hike astride mangrove-lined waterways on a groomed pathway at picturesque Lovers Key State Park. Maritime hammock vegetation lines the trail while smoothly winding through Black Island, topping one of the higher hills in Southwest Florida. Aquatic views accompany you back to the trailhead. This nexus of land and water adds to wildlife viewing possibilities.

Paddling and hiking trails run side by side at Black Island.

Distance: 2.6-mile loop
Hiking Time: 1.5 hours
Difficulty: Easy
Highlights: Maritime hardwood hammock, wildlife in adjacent waters
Cautions: Sun exposure
Fees/Permits: Entrance fee required
Best Seasons: Year-round
Other Trail Users: Bicyclists. Leashed dogs allowed.
Trail Contacts: Lovers Key State Park, 8700 Estero Boulevard, Fort Myers Beach, FL 33931, (239) 463-4588, www.floridastateparks.org
Finding the Trailhead: From exit 111 on I-75 north of Naples, take Bonita Beach Road west 10.5 miles to the main entrance to Lovers Key State Park. Continue past the entrance station, driving .7 mile to reach the Black Island Trail parking on your left.
GPS Trailhead Coordinates: N26° 23.676', W81° 52.582'

One look at the hiking-trail map of Lovers Key State Park reveals that Black Island—your hiking destination—has been altered from its natural state. A series of fingerlike canals twist and turn through the island, in a manner designed for maximum waterfront property access. Back in the 1970s, canals were dug on Black Island, and the dredge spoils were used to create land for houses. Despite Black Island being permanently altered, the state bought the soon-to-be development and merged it with Carl E. Johnson County Park to form Lovers Key State Park.

Lovers Key State Park is better known for beaches than trails. The primary Gulf beach extends for 2.5 miles and is popular with shell seekers. Spread over four barrier islands, the park is as much about the water around these islands as the land. The Gulf, the estuarine waters, and lesser wetlands attract a variety of birdlife. The park leads kayak tours and also rents boats, in addition to canoes and bicycles. Park naturalist programs are held throughout the year. Shore fishing is popular, especially on the tidal passes between islands.

The Black Island Trail travels along the aforementioned dredged canals, probably over planned roads. The State of Florida

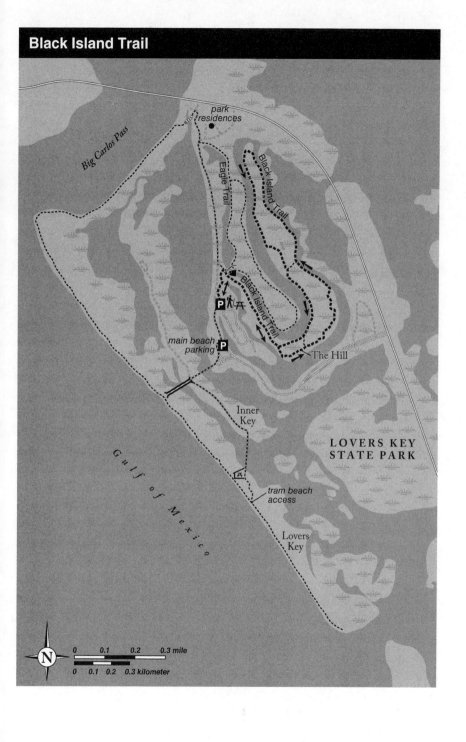

Black Island Trail

Big Carlos Pass

park residences

Eagle Trail

Black Island Trail

Black Island Trail

P

P

main beach parking

The Hill

Inner Key

Gulf of Mexico

LOVERS KEY STATE PARK

tram beach access

Lovers Key

N

0   0.1   0.2   0.3 mile

0   0.1   0.2   0.3 kilometer

has succeeded in reestablishing a maritime hammock forest on the land above the canals. Here you will hike astride sea grape, strangler fig, palm, cat's claw, and gumbo-limbo. Spanish bayonet is a spiny understory component, while coco plum is easier on the hands and legs, and offers fruits in season.

Leave the trailhead and immediately pass through a planted butterfly garden. The trail curves right, past an informative kiosk, and then reaches a trail intersection. Here, the Eagle Trail leaves left, but you stay right, joining the Black Island Trail. A fishing pier with a picnic table draws in hikers.

The packed sand trail turns south. The wide track is mostly open to the sun overhead, though the maritime hammock forest stretches farther over the trail with each passing season. Informative interpretive signs are scattered throughout the hike. Reading interpretive signs gives you a break and an education at the same time. Canals are usually visible and spur trails often lead to the water's edge where birders are eye-glassing for a heron, eagle, or osprey. You will see birds on your hike, and perhaps kayakers plying the canals.

At .4 mile, reach the loop portion of the hike. The Black Island Trail is popular with bicyclists as well as hikers; therefore the loop travels in one direction to avoid biker-hiker accidents. Make sure to stay right here, going with the flow. Surprisingly, the trail climbs a hill, topping out at .5 mile. For reasons forgotten, this spoil pile was left behind by the developers. Now, grown over with native vegetation, it seems almost natural, though any Southwest Florida resident knows that a hill this high here is man-made. The rise is known simply as The Hill.

Drop off The Hill and continue tracing the undulations of the canal off to your right. Sea-grape trees form shady tunnels. Pass a shortcut leading left. Some parts of the trail are grassy. At .8 mile, come directly alongside a canal. The trail passes a second shortcut. At 1.4 miles, the path meets the end of the peninsula it has been traversing, and turns back south. Come alongside the canal again, as it, too, has made a big bend. Continue enjoying the mix of maritime hardwoods and mangrove-lined canals.

Bird life is abundant on Black Island's waterside trails, so bring your binoculars and bird book.

At 1.7 miles, pass a spur trail leading left to a small pond, often inhabited by alligators. At 1.8 miles, pass the other end of the upper shortcut. Keep hiking south. The trail gently curves with the canals and passes the lower shortcut. At 2.2 miles, you have completed the loop portion of the Black Island Trail. Backtrack .4 mile, returning to the trailhead and finishing the hike.

Mileages at a Glance

- 0.0   Black Island Trail trailhead
- 0.4   Begin loop portion of hike, heading right
- 0.5   Scale The Hill
- 1.4   Turn south on the peninsula
- 2.2   Complete the loop
- 2.6   Return to trailhead

27

Lovers Key Trail and Beach Walk

Hike Summary: This trek starts by exploring a maritime hammock on Black Island. Then it emerges onto Lovers Key, where you take a beach walk. Overlook Big Carlos Pass and then curve south, opening onto the Gulf of Mexico. Hike along the beach of Lovers Key State Park, enjoying the natural setting. The hike

Beach walking is part of the Lovers Key hiking experience.

continues south, reaching the end of the island at New Pass. You will then backtrack, bridging Inner Key before returning to the trailhead.

Distance: 4.5-mile loop
Hiking time: 3.0 hours
Difficulty: Moderate
Highlights: Maritime hardwood hammock, protected Gulf beach
Cautions: Sun exposure, slow sand hiking
Fees/Permits: Entrance fee required
Best Seasons: Year-round
Other Trail Users: Bicyclists in places. No dogs allowed on beach.
Trail Contacts: Lovers Key State Park, 8700 Estero Boulevard, Fort Myers Beach, FL 33931, (239) 463-4588, www.floridastateparks.org
Finding the Trailhead: From exit 111 on I-75 north of Naples, take Bonita Beach Road west 10.5 miles to the main entrance to Lovers Key State Park. Continue past the entrance station, driving .7 mile to the Black Island Trail parking on your left.
GPS Trailhead Coordinates: N26° 23.676', W81° 52.582'

This hike combines two of the most scenic ecosystems of seaside Southwest Florida—maritime hardwood forests and Gulf Coast beaches. You will start at the Black Island Trail trailhead but quickly leave most hikers behind, as this hike heads north on the lesser-used Eagle Trail, but instead of doing the main loop of the Eagle Trail, the hike heads to the north end of Black Island, reaching an alternate parking area on Estero Boulevard. Here the trek evolves into a beach walk as you reach Lovers Key.

Cruise the sandy shore along the channel between Lovers Key and Estero Island. Sunbathers, boaters, and anglers will be seen here. Turn on the point of Lovers Key and head south, gaining panoramic Gulf of Mexico vistas. This upper part of the beach is walked less, and you will mostly be sharing it with the shorebirds. However, the crowds pick up as you head down the beach. Most sunbathers will be close to the beach-access points. But once again you will pass the crowds and head to the south tip of

Lovers Key Trail and Beach Walk

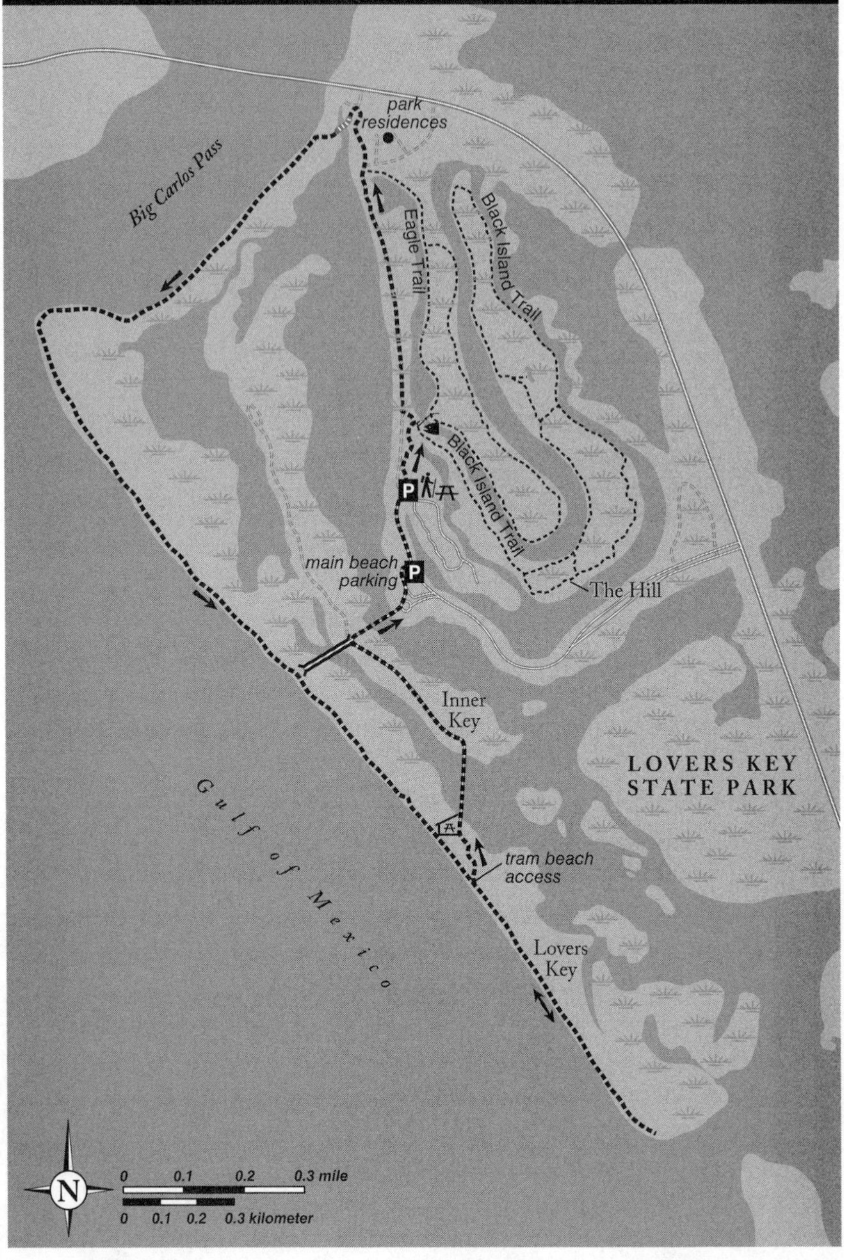

Big Carlos Pass

park residences

Eagle Trail

Black Island Trail

Black Island Trail

P

main beach parking

P

The Hill

Inner Key

LOVERS KEY STATE PARK

Gulf of Mexico

tram beach access

Lovers Key

N

| 0 | 0.1 | 0.2 | 0.3 mile |

| 0 | 0.1 | 0.2 | 0.3 kilometer |

Only the man in the picture needs a rod to catch fish.

Lovers Key, overlooking New Pass. The final part of the hike uses the beach tram road to return to Black Island and the trailhead.

Join the Black Island Trail as it passes a butterfly garden and reaches a trail junction. Here, turn left, joining a path heading north, the Eagle Trail. Shortly meet a sandy track heading north toward Big Carlos Pass. Cruise alongside mangrove to your left and maritime hammock to your right with sea grape, strangler fig, and more. At .5 miles, the main loop of the Eagle Trail leaves right. There is a park staff residence road here as well. At .6 mile, reach the alternate trailhead parking area on Estero Boulevard. Picnic tables and restrooms enhance the locale. Stay left, bridging a mangrove-lined stream to reach the beach overlooking Big Carlos Pass. You are now on Lovers Key. Cruise along the sandy shoreline where sunbathers fry and surf anglers fish. The high-tide line rises to grasses and sea oats, behind which grow sea grapes, Jamaica dogwoods, and mangroves.

Picking your hiking angle along the beach depends upon the tide. At 1.1 miles, the water and forest come together, squeezing the beach line. Past here you begin curving around the northwest tip of Lovers Key. Turn the corner and begin heading southerly. Shorebirds will be gathered on the beach, as will a few photographers and beachcombers. You will likely see active osprey nests in the vicinity. Continue south, coming to a boardwalk beach at 2.1 miles. The beach becomes busy here and you continue south, reaching the tram access to the beach at 2.5 miles. Head south, still beachcombing, into solitude again. Meet the southern tip of Lovers Key and New Pass at 3.1 miles. Look south at more islands. New Pass is a popular fishing spot as the tides run through it rapidly. Note the multicolored Gulf waters here. Backtrack up the beach, reaching the tram beach access at 3.6 miles. Trace the tram road, crossing to Inner Key. If you are really tired, get a ride on the tram. Walk across Inner Key and take another bridge to reach Black Island and the busy main-beach parking area. Turn left here, walking the park road to make the Black Island parking area at 4.4 miles.

Mileages at a Glance

- 0.0 Black Island Trail trailhead
- 0.6 Alternate parking area on Estero Boulevard
- 2.1 Pass the bridge access to the beach
- 2.5 Pass the tram access to the beach
- 3.1 Reach New Pass
- 3.6 Right onto tram access
- 4.1 Reach main beach parking area
- 4.4 Return to trailhead

28

Bird Rookery Swamp Loop

Hike Summary: This is the longest hike in this guide. It traverses some of the most remote terrain in Southwest Florida while looping through junglelike cypress-maple swamps. The good news is that the loop uses old elevated logging trams, allowing for dry-footed exploration of this wild, wooded wetland. Expect to see birdlife aplenty in the trailside landscape, in a preserved parcel of the greater Corkscrew Swamp, managed as part of the greater CREW lands, and maintained as an aquifer recharge zone.

Trailside alligators add interest to the hike.

Distance: 12.0-mile loop

Hiking time: 7.0 hours

Difficulty: Difficult

Highlights: Huge, wild swamp

Cautions: Remote terrain

Fees/Permits: No fees or permits required

Best Seasons: November through April

Other Trail Users: Bicyclists. Leashed dogs allowed.

Trail contacts: CREW Land & Water Trust, 23998 Corkscrew Road, Estero, FL 33928, (239) 657-2253, www.crewtrust.org

Finding the Trailhead: From exit 111 on I-75, travel Lee County Road 846, Immokalee Road, east for 11.4 miles to turn left on Shady Hollow Boulevard. Follow Shady Hollow Boulevard west. At 1.7 miles, the pavement ends. Continue for .4 mile farther, and the CREW Bird Rookery Swamp trailhead will be on your right.

GPS Trailhead Coordinates: N26° 18.725', W81° 38.034'

Making a 12-mile loop through a remote swamp may seem daunting to most hikers. However, there is actually nothing to fear and a beautiful experience to be gained. Part of the greater CREW Trust Lands occupying 60,000 acres in Corkscrew Swamp, Bird Rookery Swamp is a vital aquifer recharge area that doubles as a harbor for Southwest Florida's wild residents. While traversing these old tram roads, it is easy to visualize Bird Rookery Swamp as home to the Florida panther, black bear, and other secretive residents of the back of beyond, birds, too.

The entire loop is sometimes pedaled by bicyclists, but most visitors simply walk the first mile or so of the path, checking out the swamp on a boardwalk, and then turn around. However, our hike goes all the way. Leave the parking area northbound on an all-access gravel path. At .2 mile, reach the boardwalk and a signboard. Turn right here and join the elevated pathway, heading east into a wet and deep portion of Bird Rookery Swamp. Enter wet woods of bald cypress, red maple, pond apple, and alligator flag. Bromeliads and ferns cover the pale cypress trunks. Duck

Bird Rookery Swamp Loop

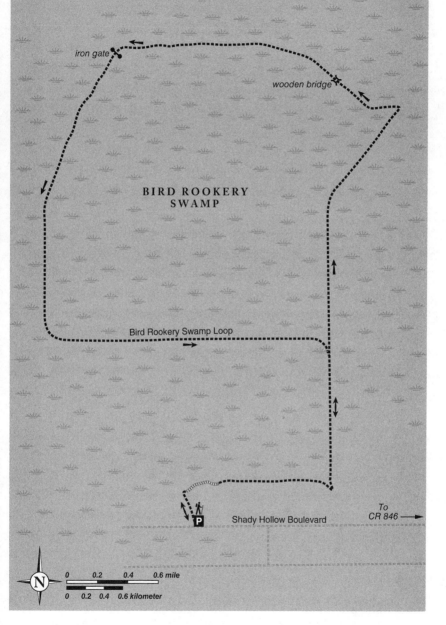

iron gate

wooden bridge

BIRD ROOKERY
SWAMP

Bird Rookery Swamp Loop

P

Shady Hollow Boulevard

To
CR 846

N

0   0.2   0.4   0.6 mile

0   0.2   0.4   0.6 kilometer

moss covers parts of the water below. Views extend deep into the primeval bayou.

Drop off the boardwalk at .4 mile; then join an elevated logging tram, beelining through the brooding depths. The trailside vegetation opens a bit, and at 1.2 miles, Saddlebrook Lake comes into view, just south of the preserve boundary. At 1.3 miles, the trail turns left, northbound. Leave Saddlebrook Lake behind at 1.5 miles, penetrating into the heart of Bird Rookery Swamp.

You will soon note spurs heading off the main tram road you are following. Each of these offshoots is marked with a sign saying "Service Road," eliminating confusion. These service roads are also overgrown and do not tempt the wandering hiker. Still other signs point the way back to the parking area.

Reach the loop portion of the hike at 2.1 miles. Here, stay straight, still northbound, under a magnificent green tunnel of deciduous swamp trees (your return route leaves left at a northwest angle). Watch for alligators in the parallel canals. Birds will fly away upon your passing. You will hear the calls of other avians echoing from the unseen distance. Bird Rookery Swamp lives up to its name. The trams were built in the 1950s, when the wetland was logged.

Continue deeper into the swamp. At 3.0 miles, the tram you are tracing deviates slightly east of due north. In places, this built-up old railroad is irregular and uneven with exposed pinnacle rock and cypress roots. The bordering swamp remains alive above and below the water line. At 3.9 miles, the loop makes an acute left turn. Here, the berm has been further built up since the logging days. The paralleling canal, bordered with willows, is larger and the trail is open overhead.

Corkscrew Swamp Sanctuary is just to your right, north. Turn northeast at 4.1 miles and resume the more primitive tram road. At 4.4 miles, span a slough on a primitive wooden bridge. Walk more of the long, green tunnel in the heart of the swamp, passing through occasional open spots. The trail angles due west at 5.0 miles. These turns are always gradual, to accommodate the logging trains that once carried incredible amounts of timber, mostly ancient cypresses, to market. Imagine that time, with noisy saws, sawdust, chugging trains with plumes of smoke rising as they plied these very rail beds we now walk. Nature has recuperated quite well in the Bird Rookery Swamp.

At 6.0 miles, bisect an old iron gate, now southbound. The swamp is so lush it recalls the southernism, "If it ain't movin', somethin's a-growing on it." Turn easterly at 8.0 miles. You are now on the home stretch. Note newer culverts added in places to facilitate increased water flow through the swamp. Birds and alligators congregate around the culvert outflows. At 9.9 miles, complete the loop part of the hike. That was a long loop—7.8 miles! From here, it is a simple 2.1 mile backtrack to the trailhead, making a 12.0-mile endeavor.

Mileages at a Glance

0.0 CREW Bird Rookery Swamp trailhead

0.2 Begin boardwalk

0.4 End boardwalk

1.3 Trail heads left, northbound

2.1 Stay straight at loop origin

3.9 Acute left on elevated berm

4.4 Cross slough on primitive wood span

6.0 Pass through iron gate, southbound

8.0 Trail heads due east

9.9 Complete the loop, backtrack

12.0 Return to trailhead

29

Corkscrew Swamp Sanctuary

Hike Summary: Take a walk through arguably one of the loveliest spots in Southwest Florida. You will travel a 2.2-mile boardwalk through the last remaining old-growth cypress swamp forest in the area, along with the other plants—and animals and birds—that call this appropriately named sanctuary home. A complete visit includes touring the visitor center and then meandering the boardwalk circuit, along with its side stops. Visit pines, palms, prairies, as well as the cypress swamp, where you

Some of the cypress trees here have stood for half a millenium.

will get deep in a slice of wildness that exceeds high expectations. Allow ample time to explore this Sunshine State treasure.

Distance: 2.2-mile loop
Hiking time: 3.0 hours
Difficulty: Easy
Highlights: Old-growth cypress forest
Cautions: None
Fees/Permits: Entrance fee required
Best Seasons: Year-round
Other Trail Users: None. No dogs allowed.
Trail contacts: Corkscrew Swamp Sanctuary, 375 Sanctuary Road, Naples, FL 34120, (239) 348-9151, www.corkscrew.audubon.org
Finding the Trailhead: From exit 111 on I-75, exit east onto Immokalee Road. Follow it for 15 miles to the signed left turn onto Sanctuary Road, Collier County 849 north. Follow it for 1.5 miles to dead-end at the sanctuary.
Other: Open 7 a.m.–5:30 p.m., year-round; no admittance after 4:30 p.m.
GPS Trailhead Coordinates: N26° 22.547', W81° 36.219'

Most Southwest Florida residents have heard of Corkscrew Swamp. It is one of those places that will likely exceed your lofty expectations for the incredible natural beauty that contains a "gentle pristine wilderness that dates back more than 500 years." That quote from the sanctuary brochure sums up this incredible swamp forest complemented by a mosaic of ecosystems that replicate much of what Southwest Florida was in days gone by.

Join the incredible boardwalk after passing through the Blair Audubon Center and paying your fee. Maintaining this 2-mile elevated deck is a continual undertaking but part of what makes the Corkscrew Swamp experience special. This privately run organization is part of the greater Audubon Society. Be prepared to share the trail with birders and photographers aplenty. The boardwalk travels counterclockwise, and you soon head left. Study the informative displays explaining the natural world

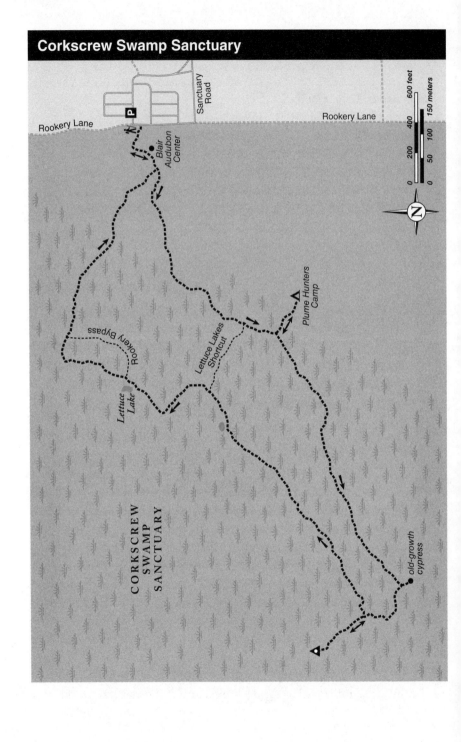

Corkscrew Swamp Sanctuary

Rookery Lane

Sanctuary Road

P

Rookery Lane

Blair Audubon Center

Plume Hunters Camp

Rookery Bypass

Lettuce Lakes Shortcut

Lettuce Lake

CORKSCREW SWAMP SANCTUARY

old-growth cypress

N

0   200   400   600 feet

0   50   100   150 meters

Ibis stalk the shallows in Corkscrew Swamp.

through which you pass, as well as historical information that puts the story of Corkscrew Swamp in perspective. Take your time reading these displays as well as simply absorbing the natural world around you—it is that exceptional.

Enjoy slash pines, cypress domes, hardwood hammocks, and willowy wetlands right off the bat. Alcoves in the boardwalk allow you to overlook plant and animal habitats, comfortably using your binoculars or camera without blocking the boardwalk. You will also pass strategically located rain shelters that protect visitors from summertime thunderstorms. Volunteer naturalists are stationed along the trail to help answer your questions. Take advantage of this rare opportunity. For them, there is not a dumb question, except the one unasked.

At .3 mile, pass the connector leading right to the Lettuce Lakes. It shortcuts the loop, and you certainly do not want to do that. Keep straight on the main boardwalk, continuing in the brooding cypress swamp, full of maples, pond apples, ferns, and of course, cypress trees. At .4 mile, take a spur leading left to the Plume Hunters Camp. You will reach dry ground where plume hunters once stayed while extracting feathers from birds of the Corkscrew Swamp, more than a century back. Ironically, the plume hunter's decimation of bird species, such as wood storks and great egrets, ultimately brought about protection of places such as Corkscrew Swamp.

At .7 mile, the boardwalk enters the heart of the old-growth cypress swamp. It seems otherworldly, or from another time. The colossal trees covered in resurrection ferns, the cypress knees upon which ferns grow, and the royal palms adding stately elegance—this is Florida in its most magnificent finery. At 1.0 mile, a spur leaves up an elevated boardwalk to a raised platform overlooking a willow marsh. Here, grasses, water, and willows stretch outward, framed by taller trees in the distance.

Return to the intimate swamp, continuing along the boardwalk through the cypress giants. The more you look, the more of the cypress swamp forest you see—small details, such as wood grains, or tiny wildflowers, or the shape of a pond-apple leaf.

Come to open wetlands at 1.4 miles. Here, birds congregate to feed. As water levels lower, birds and reptiles share shrinking waters, concentrating wildlife. At 1.5 miles, the Lettuce Lakes shortcut comes in on your right. Keep straight on the boardwalk, coming to Lettuce Lakes. Photographers gather here to shoot pictures in this wetter area of the swamp.

At 1.6 miles, a bypass trail avoids nesting wood storks in season. Corkscrew hosts the largest colony of nesting wood storks in the United States. You will continue through relatively more open swamp and then reach the other end of the bypass. Bisect a stand of much younger cypress trees, markedly different than the ancient cypress stand of earlier. Cross an open wetland and then join pinelands for your final jaunt back to the trailhead.

Mileages at a Glance

- 0.0 Blair Audubon Center trailhead
- 0.3 Spur leads right to Lettuce Lakes, stay left
- 0.4 Left spur to Plume Hunters Camp
- 0.7 Enter heart of old-growth swamp
- 1.0 Left spur to Marsh Overlook
- 1.6 Nesting wood stork Bypass
- 2.2 Return to trailhead

30

Barefoot Beach Preserve Hike

Hike Summary: Enjoy this exemplary Southwest Florida barrier-island trek. Start by walking the Saylor Trail through coastal maritime woodland mixed with saltwater mangrove forest. Emerge at sandy Wiggins Pass and then beach walk along the Gulf, combing the sand, where tides affect your exact route. Return to the maritime forest, exploring the heart of the isle of Barefoot Beach, back on the Saylor Trail. A woodland backtrack returns you to the trailhead.

They don't call it Barefoot Beach Preserve for nothing.

Distance: 3.0-mile balloon loop
Hiking time: 2.0 hours
Difficulty: Moderate
Highlights: Maritime forest, Wiggins Pass, beachcombing
Cautions: Excessive sun exposure
Fees/Permits: Entrance fee required
Best Seasons: November through April; beach year-round
Other Trail Users: None. No dogs allowed on beach.
Trail Contacts: Collier County Parks, 3299 Tamiami Trail East, Naples, FL 34112, (239) 252-8999, colliergov.net
Finding the Trailhead: From exit 116 on I-75, take Bonita Beach Road, Lee County Road 865 west for 5.7 miles to a traffic light and Barefoot Beach Boulevard. Turn left on Barefoot Beach Boulevard, passing through a residential area, and follow it for 1.6 miles to dead-end at the preserve entrance station. Continue for .5 mile beyond the entrance station to Beach Access #3. Circle around to the very back of the loop road and pick up the Saylor Trail.
GPS Trailhead Coordinates: N26° 17.996', W81° 49.976'

Explore the three primary components of a barrier-island ecosystem on this hike—coastal maritime hammock woodland, estuarine mangrove woodland, and coastal beach. Pass around a gate and join an old shell road amid tightly knit palms and sea grapes on the Saylor Trail. You can see the tidal waters of Back Bay to your left, through a partial mangrove screen. Cruise south, soaking in the scads of interpretive signs identifying the plants that occupy this 342-acre preserve with both Gulf and bay frontage, quite valuable land. Once a state park, it was deeded over to Collier County, which now manages it.

As you hike, notice the ancient, now-wooded dunes to your right, providing vertical variation to the barrier island. Gumbo-limbo, Jamaica dogwood, coco plum, and other freshwater species populate the former dunes. Parts of the trail open to the sun overhead can be sandy and slow. At .6 mile, reach a trail intersection. The main loop of the Saylor Trail leaves right, but for now, stay straight, south, heading for Wiggins Pass. Continue

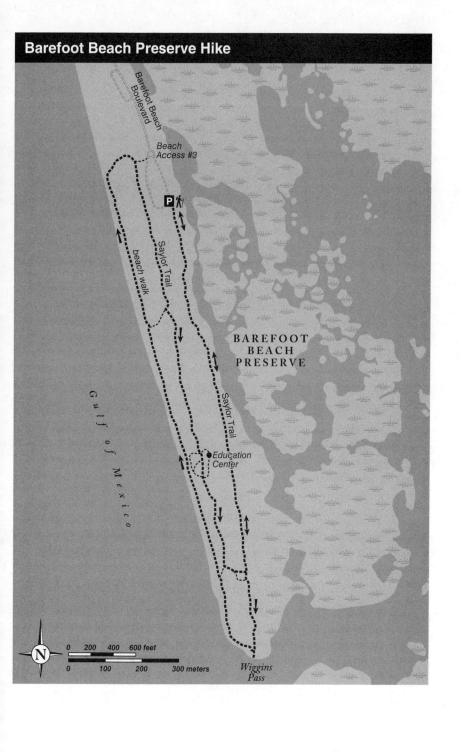

Barefoot Beach Preserve Hike

Barefoot Beach Boulevard

Beach Access #3

P

Saylor Trail

beach walk

BAREFOOT
BEACH
PRESERVE

Saylor Trail

Education
Center

Gulf of Mexico

0   200   400   600 feet
0   100   200   300 meters

N

Wiggins Pass

Wiggins Pass is an interesting meeting place of sea and shore.

in forest until it opens onto blinding-white beach. Ahead blue-green Gulf waters pass back and forth through Wiggins Pass, an aquatic flow linking Back Bay and the Gulf. The spot is popular with visitors for its shelling, fishing, birding, and boating. Delnor-Wiggins Pass State Park is just across the water, effectively adding to the natural acreage.

Curve right, away from Wiggins Pass, tracing the sand along the Gulf, now northbound. Visually endless waters stretch west to the horizon. Follow a sandy strip separating the maritime forest from the Gulf. Squawking birds and silent shells dot the sands. Condos rise in the distant sky, contrasting with the preserve. Sea oats wave on the immediate shore, framed by wind-molded sea-grape trees.

Most beach visitors will congregate around the closest auto-accessible beach accesses. At 1.6 miles, turn in on Beach Access #3, among sun worshippers and swimmers. Look for the sign R-12, indicating Beach Access #3. Join a boardwalk and then quickly reach the Saylor Trail again. Come within mere feet of the parking area for Beach Access #3, but turn right, rejoining the Saylor Trail. This segment takes you through the heart of the island, southbound again. In places, the forest gives way to barren salt flats, where overwash from the high-water events leaves the land infertile.

At 1.9 miles, reach a bench memorializing the trail's originator, Alice Saylor. She deserves recognition. The trail we hike was just an overgrown shell road until the Friends of Barefoot Beach Preserve, of which Alice Saylor was a member, stepped in. They cleared the roadbed, removed exotic vegetation, and added interpretive signage to help identify the rich array of trailside plants. At 2.2 miles, pass by a restroom and a spur trail to the park education center. At 2.4 miles, turn east; then meet the Saylor Trail segment where you were earlier, near Wiggins Pass. From here it is but .6 mile back to the trailhead.

Mileages at a Glance

0.0 South end of Barefoot Beach Preserve Beach Access #3

0.6 Intersection, stay straight toward Wiggins Pass

1.6 Right at Beach Access #3, right on Saylor Trail

2.2 Spur to education center

2.4 Intersection, backtrack left to trailhead

3.0 Return to Beach Access #3

31

Clam Pass Park

Hike Summary: Located near downtown Naples, this park is popular with both residents and area visitors. From the parking area, you will follow a wide boardwalk through mangrove forest. Soak in a view of a tidal stream on a high bridge. The trail then dips to meet the Gulf, where beach walking extends in both directions. Additionally, park facilities include a Gulfside restaurant and a passenger tram in case you do not feel like walking back to the parking area.

This elevated boardwalk tunnels through a canopy of mangrove.

Distance: 1.2-mile there-and-back trail, excluding beach walking
Hiking Time: 1.0–1.5 hours
Difficulty: Easy
Highlights: Boardwalk, Gulf access
Cautions: Passenger tram on boardwalk
Fees/Permits: Entrance fee required
Best Seasons: Year-round
Other Trail Users: Passenger tram. No dogs allowed.
Trail Contacts: Collier County Parks and Recreation, 15000 Livingston Road, Naples FL 34109, (239) 252-4000, www.colliergov.net
Finding the Trailhead: From exit 107, Naples/Golden Gate, on I-75, take Collier County 896, Pine Ridge Road, west for 3.9 miles to US 41. Here, stay straight through the light as the road turns to Seagate Drive. Follow it straight to shortly dead-end into Clam Pass Park. After entering the park, the boardwalk starts on your right as you enter.
GPS Trailhead Coordinates: N26° 12.686', W81° 48.706'

Most area residents do not think of Clam Pass Park as a hiking destination. However, it is a beach destination for many a visitor to Southwest Florida. The park presents oceanside access very near downtown Naples on its 35 acres of high-dollar property. The elevated boardwalk presents a midforest-level perspective of the mangrove forest, lying between the parking area and the beach. At a high point, you can look over the tidal creek linking Outer Clam Bay to the Gulf.

The trail's end at the Gulf of Mexico is unlike almost all hiking endpoints. Here, atop a sand hill overlooking the ocean, you will find a restaurant, restrooms, and a booth offering beach rentals such as chairs and shade umbrellas. And then, if you eat too much or walk your legs silly on the beach, tram drivers will gladly carry you back to the parking lot! Admittedly, there have been a few hikes in my life where a ride would have been welcome.

Leaving the parking area, do not be tempted by the tram drivers offering rides on demand to the beach on the wide boardwalk. At least walk at the outset. However, these trams—long,

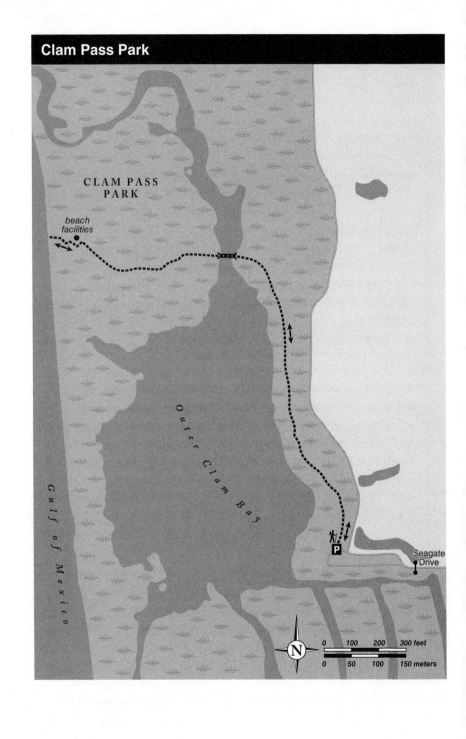

Clam Pass Park

CLAM PASS
PARK

beach
facilities

Outer Clam Bay

Gulf of Mexico

P

Seagate
Drive

N

| 0 | 100 | 200 | 300 feet |
| 0 | 50 | 100 | 150 meters |

The Gulf lies at boardwalk's end.

multiseat golf carts—are popular with visitors, especially those going to the beach and toting gear. Leave the parking area and immediately join the boardwalk, heading north in red mangrove, black mangrove, and buttonwood. Some of the trees are huge for their species. Note the gigantic leatherferns growing near the bases of the coastal trees. Look down at the intertwined prop roots of the red mangrove and the nutrient-rich muck from which the forest rises. The boardwalk is about midlevel with the trees, allowing the unusual perspective.

The boardwalk is very wide, allowing passage of the trams and visitors aplenty, yet it is partly shaded. The boardwalk then begins heading upward, and at .4 mile you emerge from the mangroves and now overlook the tidal creek connecting Clam Pass to Clam Pass Bay. Your above-treeline view also reveals the numerous high-rises that line this part of the coast. It is hard to believe that just over a half century back Naples was a sleepy fishing village. The Calusa Indians never could have imagined this!

Descend from the tidal stream, back into mangrove. At .6 mile, arrive at a turnaround. Here, you cut through the restaurant, restroom building, and descend to the Gulf beach on a boardwalk. Down here, a hut with beach-rental stands. More important, an alluring swath of sand extends north and south, a white linear hiking trail if you will, where the sights, smells, and sounds of the Gulf and the land that lines it provide a natural aspect that accompanies all the people-watching and checking out of properties in this part of Southwest Florida.

How far you walk on the beach depends on you. Enjoy. One more thing: Guided nature walks are given at Clam Pass Park on a regular basis. Check the park website for dates and times to coordinate your visit.

Mileages at a Glance

0.0 Clam Pass Park trailhead
0.4 Bridge over tidal stream
0.6 Beachfront facilities
1.2 Return to trailhead

32

Lasip Mitigation Park

Hike Summary: This restored slice of wild Florida offers area residents a loop trail through pines, palms, and wildlife at a nearly 100-acre parcel of land encircled by development. Enjoy this circuit, full of interpretive information about how once-compromised terrain has been restored to its original finery, becoming an oasis for man and beast, and a tool in managing storm water in Collier County.

Restored pine flatwoods at Lasip Park mitigate urban runoff.

Distance: 1.1-mile loop
Hiking Time: 1.0 hours
Difficulty: Easy
Highlights: Restored pine-palm-cypress community
Cautions: None
Fees/Permits: No fees or permits required
Best Seasons: November through April; open 7 a.m. to dusk
Other Trail Users: None. No dogs allowed.
Trail Contacts: Collier County, 3299 Tamiami Trail East, Naples, FL 34112, (239) 252-8999, www.colliergov.net
Finding the Trailhead: From exit 101 on I-75 east of Naples, take Collier County Road 951, Collier Boulevard South, for 2.5 miles to the right turn into Lasip Mitigation Park. Keep your eyes peeled because the right turn is quick and the parking lot small.
GPS Trailhead Coordinates: N26° 7.34′, W81° 41.21′

Most hikers drive by Lasip Mitigation Park without knowing it's there. I discovered it when I was driving by on busy Collier Boulevard, in the stream of traffic, and noticed the park sign. I pulled in and went on an impromptu investigative walk. A small, elevated picnic area greeted me from the small parking area. The short hike made for an enjoyable morning exercise. I recommend the same for you.

The odd name Lasip is an acronym that stands for Lely Area Stormwater Improvement Plan. An 11,000-acre drainage basin, mostly developed, had no organized drainage, resulting in regular flooding. Canals, culverts, and overflow lakes were constructed to improve storm-water runoff, which resulted in the loss of wetlands. Collier County purchased this tract to offset those wetland losses and help soak in rain. This is known as mitigation. While original native wetlands are always preferred, sometimes it is not feasible to save them. Thus, we end up with tracts such as this.

After purchasing a mitigation tract, Collier County restores undeveloped lands to their native state, removing exotic vegetation and refurbishing the original hydrology. When the property

Lasip Mitigation Park

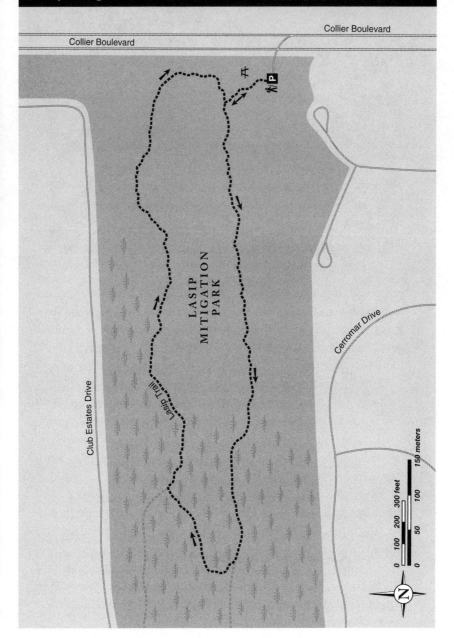

was purchased in 2007, it was full of melaleuca and other exotic vegetation, and it offered little for Florida's native wildlife. Today the property has been restored to a mix of cypress wetlands, wet pine flatwoods, and upland pinelands. Much of the native flora was planted in 2009 and is thriving today, and the birds and the beasts have returned.

Leave the parking area off busy Collier Boulevard and dip into the tract. You will immediately pass the aforementioned picnic area, along with an informative trail map. Tall pines rise overhead. Palms find their place in the shadows of the pines. Palmettos form low thickets.

The wide, grassy path shortly reaches the loop portion of the hike. Soak in the interpretive signage explaining the whole water-mitigation process. It is a costly endeavor, but Southwest Florida is going in a more environmentally sensible direction after seeing the mistakes made by the east coast megalopolis of Fort Lauderdale/Miami. It makes practical sense to preserve oases of nature while minimizing the impact of large populations as Southwest Florida grows.

Make your loop clockwise, heading left, westerly, underneath brown trunks of pine swaying in the wind, their green, needle-covered branches backlit by the sky. Soil, needles, and sand form a soft trail bed at your feet. Coco plums rise in bushes. Cypress trees grow here as well, and in summertime the path may be wet; it's probably buggy, too. I wouldn't hike here then. The circuit makes the most of the rectangular parcel. At .2 mile, the trail narrows and becomes more of a traditional hiking path.

Look overhead for woodpeckers. You will likely hear their knocking sounds, despite the din from Collier Boulevard. Occasional open grassy areas, seasonal wetlands, add another perspective to the tract. You can see the tract's north and south boundaries, where houses rise above the understory. For me, that does not detract from the scenery; instead, it attests to the value of a park in a developed area where we can hike and be in nature.

At .5 mile, the trail curves back toward the trailhead. Wetland mitigation was also executed in this area, creating seasonally inundated areas to replace ones lost by development. In wintertime, the wetland may simply seem a bunch of grass with scattered cypress trees, but come rainy season there will be plenty of standing water. Looking at the area now, it is hard to imagine this land once covered with melaleuca, Brazilian pepper, and other exotics. Fern fields rise under cypress and pine, adding to the vegetational variety. All too soon you're near Collier Boulevard again and returning to the trailhead. Since the hike is but a little over one mile, consider making a second loop. You will see more the second time around.

Mileages at a Glance

- 0.0 Lasip Mitigation Park trailhead
- 0.1 Begin loop portion of hike, heading left, westerly
- 0.5 Loop turns back east
- 1.0 Complete loop portion of hike
- 1.1 Return to trailhead

33

Duncan Trail

Hike Summary: Take a walk through important Florida panther habitat on this easy-to-access trail. First, enjoy a rich hardwood hammock; then take off among pine flatwoods and seasonal wetlands, including a shaded bird observation shelter overlooking a pond. The path works its way back to the trailhead, mixing in more oaks and pines. Since the trail is short, make sure to add the entire all-access loop through the hammock.

Shaded wildlife observation platform.

Distance: 1.4-mile loop
Hiking Time: 1.0 hours
Difficulty: Easy
Highlights: Diverse panther habitat
Cautions: Potentially wet trail during rainy season
Fees/Permits: No fees or permits required
Best Seasons: November through April; open sunrise to sunset via electronic gate
Other trail users: None. No dogs allowed.
Trail Contacts: Florida Panther National Wildlife Refuge, 3860 Tollgate Boulevard, Naples, FL 34114, (239) 353-8442, www.fws.gov/floridapanther/
Finding the Trailhead: From exit 80 on I-75 east of Naples, take FL 29 north just a short distance to reach the trailhead on your left.
GPS Trailhead Coordinates: N26° 9.703', W81° 20.773'

Though most of us will never feel the thrill of seeing a panther in the wild, it is exciting to know that much of the panther's Southwest Florida habitat is being protected so the cat can go about the business of being a panther. The Duncan Trail travels through one of these preserves, the aptly named Florida Panther National Wildlife Refuge.

The 26,000-acre refuge was established in 1989. It protects a large part of the Fakahatchee Strand of the Big Cypress Swamp. The refuge's proximity to Everglades National Park and Big Cypress National Preserve helps create a contiguous habitat area for panthers. It is estimated that at any given time five to eleven Florida panthers are using the preserve. The preserve also provides an umbrella for a host of other species, from notables such as black bear to rare orchids to lesser-known species.

The primary goal of the refuge is to provide optimum habitat for Florida panthers; public recreation is secondary. Refuge visitors are restricted to the southeastern corner of the refuge, where this hike is located. Habitat restoration to improve the ecosystem is ongoing. Refuge managers use prescribed fire and

Duncan Trail

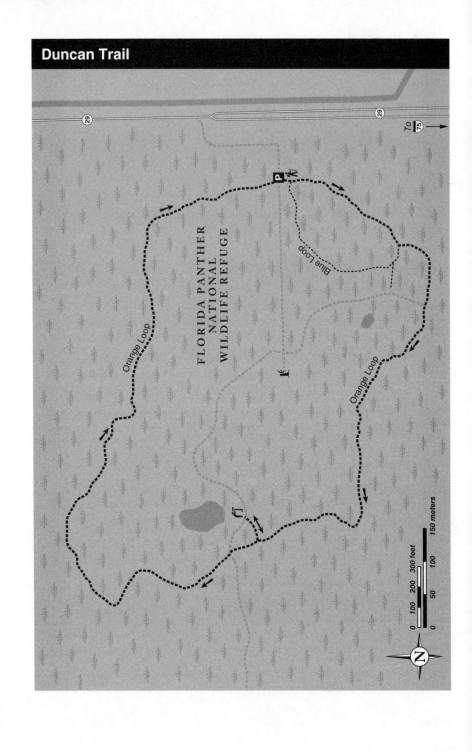

other techniques to maintain the historic natural ecosystem, as well as to control non-native flora and fauna.

Interestingly, access to the trailhead is through an electronic gate that opens and closes with sunrise and sunset. I have arrived before sunrise and could not help but wonder if the gate would open without someone around to physically open it. Sure enough, it opened at sunrise. Morning and evening are the best times to observe wildlife at the refuge. Do not expect to see the elusive panther, however. It is a rare event indeed to see a panther in the wild. After years of roaming South Florida's wildlands, I have seen only one, and I consider that a fortunate coincidence.

Leave south from the trailhead, passing through another gate, joining the Leslie M. Duncan Memorial Trail. Immediately enter a verdant hardwood hammock. The shorter Blue Loop leaves right; it circles through the hardwood hammock. Stay straight on the longer Orange Loop, enjoying some of the lush vegetation under live oaks, pines, and palms, along with ferns and other understory vegetation.

At .1 mile, stay left with the Orange Loop, which becomes a natural-surface trail. Note the exposed limestone marl as you enter more open terrain, with an open, wetland prairie on your left and a live oak/palm/laurel forest on your right. These grassy seasonal wetlands are also known as swales. Swales form a saucer-shaped depression in the land where water naturally collects during the rainy season and then dries over the winter. The standing water then seeps into the underground aquifer, from which local residents get their drinking water.

At .5 mile, the Orange Trail turns north. The surrounding forest is primarily pine and palmetto. At .6 mile, make sure to take the spur trail leading right to a covered observation shelter overlooking a seasonal pond. Take a seat on one of the benches and let the wildlife come to you. Your chances for seeing birds will increase with the level of the water in the pond, which can nearly dry up by spring, before the afternoon thunderstorms bring rain again.

Resume the loop in classic pine flatwoods, meandering north, then east. A hat and sunscreen come in handy here. At .9 mile, the trail turns decidedly easterly. Continue in pine land until 1.2 miles, when you reenter the hardwood hammock located near the trailhead. The cool, shady, leaf-covered path provides great contrast to the open pinelands. Whatever the weather, you will feel the moderating influence of the covered hardwood hammock. If the pinelands are cool, it will feel warmer in the hammock. Conversely, if the pinelands are warm; it will feel cooler in the hammock.

Emerge onto the trailhead at 1.3 miles. I suggest taking in the .3 mile all-access Blue Loop before you leave the refuge. This easy path is also child- and stroller-friendly.

Mileages at a Glance

0.0 Leslie M. Duncan Trail trailhead
0.1 Head left, staying with the Orange Trail
0.6 Spur leaves right to observation shelter
1.3 Return to trailhead

34

Sabal Palm Trail

Hike Summary: This double-loop hike explores the back of beyond at Picayune State Forest. The Sabal Palm Trail discovers a world far removed from Naples, despite being close to civilization. Wander through whispering pine forests before crossing a long cypress strand. Begin your first loop exploring other environs, from open meadows to live oak hammocks. An elevated logging tram adds perspective on your second loop. Look for deer and bear scat along the way or, better yet, the live animals that live here.

This cypress strand is wet in summer.

Distance: 3.5-mile double loop
Hiking Time: 2.0 hours
Difficulty: Moderate
Highlights: Solitude, multiple ecotones
Cautions: None
Fees/Permits: Day-use fee required
Best Seasons: November through April
Other Trail Users: None. Leashed dogs allowed.
Trail Contacts: Picayune Strand State Forest, 2121 52nd Avenue SE, Naples, FL 34117, (239) 348-7557, www.floridaforestservice.com
Finding the Trailhead: From exit 101 on I-75 east of Naples, take Collier County Road 951, Collier Boulevard South, for 4.3 miles to the left turn (no traffic light) onto Sabal Palm Road. Follow Sabal Palm Road for 3.2 miles (it turns to gravel after .9 mile) and look on your right for a signed spur road leading right to the trailhead.
GPS Trailhead Coordinates: N26° 5.63', W81° 38.08'

Part of the Florida State Forest Trailwalker Program, the Sabal Palm Trail provides your best opportunity for hiking in Picayune State Forest. Located in the old South Golden Gate Estates down US 41, this area is also known as "The Blocks" and a few other names. In the 1960s, in a classic Florida land fraud, a developer bought more than 50,000 acres of logged-over seasonal wetlands, cut canals and paved roads, and then sold undevelopable lots. The State of Florida stepped in and is still in the process of purchasing back the land—more than 17,000, tracts. Once the land purchases are complete, Picayune State Forest will restore natural flows through the swamp, connecting interior freshwater wetlands with the estuaries of the Ten Thousand Islands and coast. The forest also offers hunting, fishing, horseback riding, and primitive car camping.

Be apprised that the Sabal Palm Trail occasionally goes off and on sand roads, but all turns are well marked and signed, a breeze to follow. Fall hikers may find the path inundated in places. Winter and early spring offer dry footing. A signboard and restroom greet you at the parking area. Pass around a gate, hiking a blazed

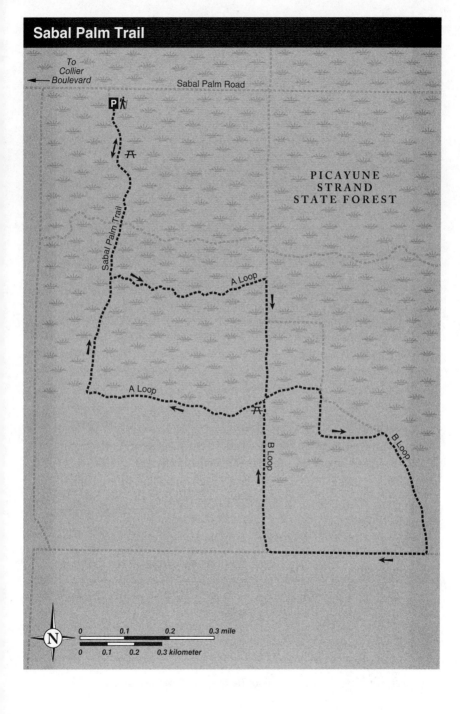

Close-up view of cypress needles.

track of pines with palmetto/wax myrtle understory. The upland path winds through evergreens to reach a small, shaded picnic area. Continue straight, making a slight descent. Here, the forest deviates to cypress, and you cross a strand where, in winter, you'll find a sea of stark white trunks from which spring a multitude of short, naked limbs.

At .4 mile, reach the first trail intersection. Here, the poorly named A Loop leaves left, traveling easterly through mixed cypress, pine, dahoon holly, and hardwoods. Despite extensive exotic removal, a few melaleuca remain. Suddenly you are in a world detached from the crowded coastal craziness of cars. Listen to the pines whoosh in the wind; see the interplay of sun and shade and spot songbirds. At .8 mile, reach the first sand road. Turn right, southbound on this well-marked turn. The path quickly leaves the sand road and keeps south, rising to an upland mix of pines and live oaks.

At 1.0 miles, meet a four-way intersection, complemented by a picnic table. This makes for a good resting and observation spot. After your break, turn left, beginning the B Loop. When hiking, scan for deer tracks in the sand or wet areas and look for acorn-laden bear scat. White-banded woodpecker nesting trees may be seen as well. Ahead, circle by a grassy area, hiking easterly. This altered landscape is now prairie-like, its former use unknown.

Arrows, blazes, and signs keep you on the right track. At 1.4 miles, the B Loop turns south again on another sand road, this one shaded by tall trees. The walking is easy. At 1.7 miles, turn right, joining an elevated logging berm. The raised path delivers a different perspective on the surroundings. Since ground was scooped to make the berm, a canal runs parallel to the track, and may have water in it, adding a year-round aquatic element to the hike.

Abruptly leave right from the berm at 2.1 miles, dipping north on the B Loop. Meander through mixed woods at that perfect elevation where it is not too dry for pure pines, or low enough to be dominated by cypress. At 2.4 miles, return to the four-way intersection, perhaps relaxing at the picnic table before finishing out the A Loop. Head left, westerly. Make your final turn north at 2.9 miles, walking amid a cypress forest on a needle and packed-sand footpath. Find bromeliads nestled in the crooks of cypresses. At 3.1 miles, you have completed both loops. Backtrack to the trailhead.

Mileages at a Glance

- 0.0 Sabal Palm Trail trailhead
- 0.1 Picnic area with table
- 0.4 Left at intersection on A Loop
- 1.0 Reach four-way intersection with picnic table, turn left
- 1.7 Turn right, westbound on an elevated logging berm
- 2.1 Leave right, north, from the berm
- 2.4 Complete the B Loop at four-way intersection, turn left on A Loop
- 3.1 Complete the A Loop. Keep straight, backtracking north toward the trailhead
- 3.5 Return to trailhead

35

Rookery Bay Hike

Hike Summary: Explore the landward side of this coastal area, mostly an aquatic preserve covering a significant swath of the Ten Thousand Islands. Start your hike at the impressive headquarters, housing a visitor center, research center, and education center. The hike leaves the visitor center, spanning mangrove-lined Henderson Creek. Descend to a streamside hammock. View an old settler homesite before circling out to fire-dependent slash-pine woods. Return to the hammock before backtracking on the view-delivering bridge over Henderson Creek.

Bridge view of a kayaker plying Henderson Creek.

Distance: 1.4-mile loop
Hiking Time: 1.5 hours
Difficulty: Easy
Highlights: Settler homesite, hardwood hammock, stellar visitor center
Cautions: None
Fees/Permits: Entrance fee required
Best Seasons: November through April; winter hours 9 a.m.-4 p.m.
Other Trail Users: None. No dogs allowed.
Trail Contacts: Rookery Bay National Estuarine Research Preserve, 300 Tower Road, Naples, FL 34113, (239) 417-6310, www.rookerybay.org
Finding the Trailhead: From exit 101 on I-75, take Collier County Road 951 south 6.9 miles to US 41. At this intersection, keep straight through the light, now on Collier Boulevard, FL 951. Continue for .6 mile; then turn right on Tower Road. Follow Tower Road for .1 mile; then turn left into the reserve headquarters. You must pass through the visitor center to access the Snail Trail.
GPS Trailhead Coordinates: N26° 2.9918', W81° 42.0573'

The complete name of this destination is Rookery Bay National Estuarine Research Reserve. Covering 110,000 acres of mostly mangrove estuaries, the reserve protects environmentally critical parts of the Greater Everglades ecosystem.

First, head to the visitor center, pay your entrance fee, and then explore the vast resources contained within, from videos to interpretive displays to historical information. Guided walks are conducted on a regular basis.

Oddly, this hike starts on the second floor of the visitor center. Here, you pick up the Snail Trail as it crosses high above Henderson Creek. Look down the waterway and across the mangroves while spanning the tidal stream. Reach dry land at .1 mile. Stay right here, making a counterclockwise loop. Enjoy a rich, shadowy forest of slash pine, live oak, and palm hammock. The trail runs roughly parallel with Henderson Creek, flowing with the tides, off to your right, veiled by a tangle of mangrove. After a quarter mile, the trail splits. Here, you can go right, to a

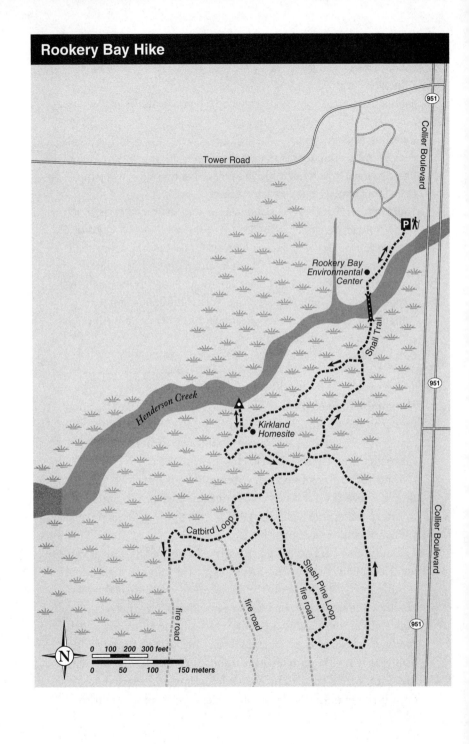

Rookery Bay Hike

Tower Road

Collier Boulevard

951

Rookery Bay Environmental Center

Snail Trail

Henderson Creek

Kirkland Homesite

Catbird Loop

Slash Pine Loop

fire road

fire road

fire road

951

951

Collier Boulevard

N

0   100   200   300 feet

0   50   100   150 meters

Your hike begins after walking through these doors.

boardwalk view of Henderson Creek, but before that, look left for an old concrete cistern marking the Kirkland homesite.

Here, land-grant settlers in the early 1900s reached this then-remote country. The 1860s Homestead Act made land here in Southwest Florida cheap and available. The Kirklands bought their 100-acre parcel for twenty-five cents an acre. They built a rough-hewn cabin with local materials, cleared land for farming and cattle grazing, made fences, and constructed the cistern to collect water for home use. The land may have been cheap, but life was tough back then. Roads were few, and access to markets was limited. It was the land of make do or do without. The Kirklands lived off their crops and livestock, and supplemented it with fish and shellfish from Henderson Creek. Storms often flooded the land, mosquitoes were ever-present, and the heat was brutal. Despite the challenges, other settlers joined the Kirklands, and this area became known as Little Marco. At this time Florida was the most rural state in the South, and much of it was still wild. It is sometimes hard to imagine the changes that Southwest Florida has undergone the last century.

While overlooking Henderson Creek, imagine the Kirkland clan and other locals using the stream for bathing and transportation—and food. Continue the Snail Trail, looping back easterly to a trail junction at .4 mile. Head right here on the "Primitive Trails." You will first pick up the Catbird Loop. This area is much more open, with scattered pines, palmetto, and prairie, which is burned on a regular basis. Fire is an important tool in Rookery Bay's arsenal to keep its acreage as natural as possible. Walk the natural-surface path, staying with the signs for the Catbird Loop, passing a couple of fire roads. At .8 mile, reach the Slash Pine Loop. Turn right here, southbound under evergreens. Wind south; then come near to Collier Boulevard at 1.0 mile, oddly peering into the back of roadside businesses. Rejoin the Snail Trail at 1.3 miles. Soak in the shady scenery before finishing the circuit and returning to the bridge over Henderson Creek. Span the tidal stream one last time, completing the hike.

Mileages at a Glance

0.0   Rookery Bay Visitor Center
0.1   Begin Snail Trail loop
0.2   Kirkland homesite
0.4   Right on Catbird Loop
0.8   Right on Slash Pine Loop
1.2   Resume Snail Trail
1.4   Return to Rookery Bay Visitor Center

36

Collier-Seminole Hiking Adventure Trail

Hike Summary: This challenging trail loops through secluded terrain at Collier-Seminole State Park. Travel among an array of environments, from pine-palm forests to wet cypress strands to hardwood hammocks. The path remains singletrack nearly throughout. Backpackers will be heartened to know a campsite lies along a spur path, offering overnighting opportunities. Expect to get your feet wet and do some mud slopping on this wild walk, whether you spend the night out here or not.

Swamp slogging is part of the fun on this hike.

Distance: 7.4-mile loop, including spur to backcountry campsite

Hiking Time: 4.5 hours

Difficulty: Difficult

Highlights: Wild Everglades woodlands, backpacking possibilities

Cautions: Muddy path, wet trail in places

Fees/Permits: Entrance fee and hiking permit required

Best Seasons: December through March

Other Trail Users: None. Leashed dogs allowed.

Trail Contacts: Collier-Seminole State Park, 20200 East Tamiami Trail, Naples, FL 34114, (239) 394-3397, www.floridastateparks.org

Finding the Trailhead: From the intersection of US 41 and Collier County Road 951 (Collier Boulevard) on the south end of Naples, drive south on US 41 for 7.6 miles. Enter the state park on your right. Head to the ranger station, fill out your permit, and get the combination to the locked parking area. Return to US 41 and head south for .5 mile. Look left for the turn onto the signed trailhead road. Open the combination gate and continue .2 mile to dead-end at the trailhead.

GPS Trailhead Coordinates: N25° 59.402', W81° 34.705'

This trail is aptly named. It can be an adventure, for backpackers and day hikers. There is a lot of wildlife out here. I have seen bear tracks and live deer and hogs. The path is well marked and signed but does cross occasional service roads; just stay with the blazes. Expect to get your feet wet on this circuit, and to step over occasional fallen trees. Whatever you do, do not come here in the summer—it will be a wet, bug-infested torture chamber.

Join the singletrack blazed Hiking Adventure Trail leaving right from the trailhead, amid scrub oaks, palms, palmetto, live oak, and wax myrtle. The forestscape will continually morph throughout the hike, one of the beauties of this hike.

At .1 mile, reach an intersection and the loop portion of the hike. Stay right here, walking counterclockwise. Before long, you enter a cypress strand rising over leatherferns and begin a little swamp slogging. The cypress soon gives way to pines and sawgrass, typical of this ever-changing wildland. At 1.7 miles, the

Collier-Seminole Hiking Adventure Trail

Tamiami Canal

41

P

Hiking Adventure Trail

Tamiami Canal

41

To Naples

Old San Marco Road

CR 92

main park entrance

COLLIER-SEMINOLE STATE PARK

N

0   0.1   0.2   0.3 mile
0   0.1 0.2 0.3 kilometer

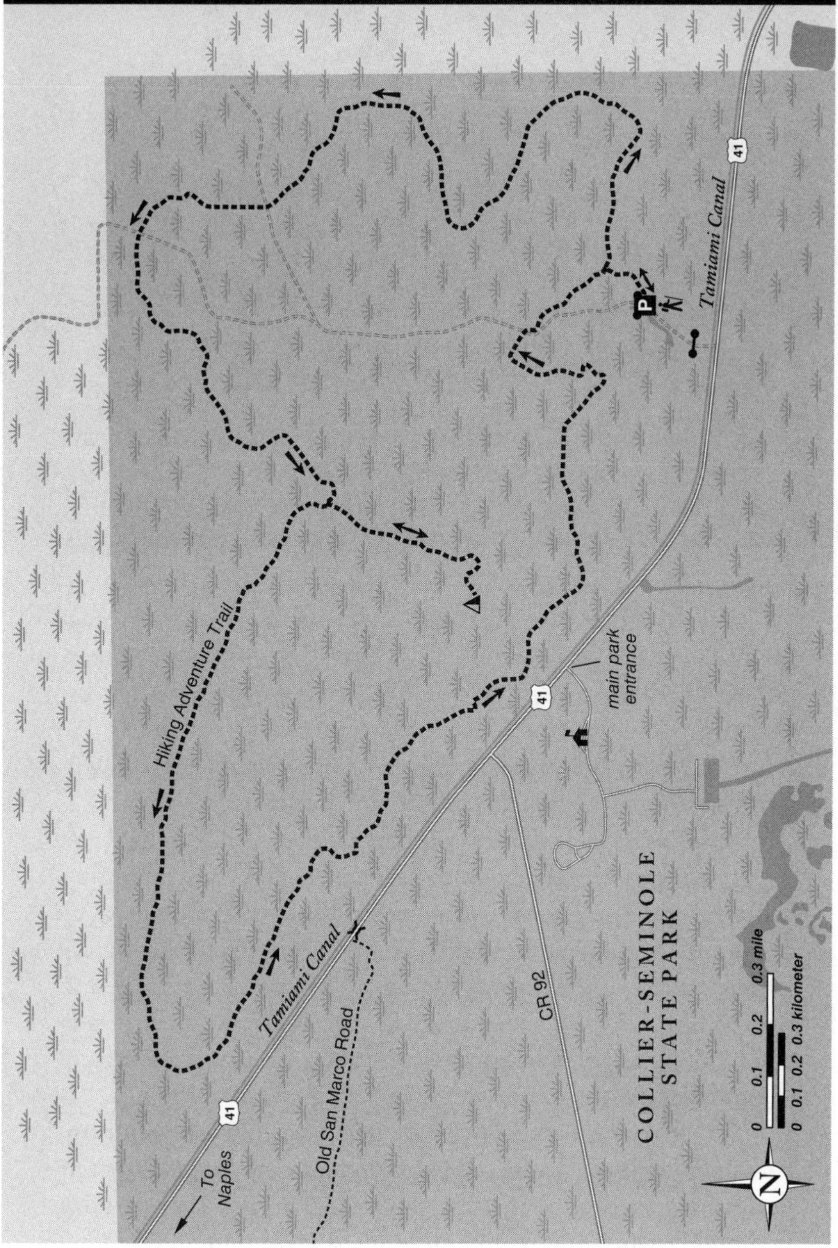

Colorful
flora com-
plements
the fauna
found deep
in these
woods.

Hiking Adventure Trail crosses a service road and keeps north, crossing a small prairie to find a cypress strand. The trail becomes lower and wetter. Note the alligator flag, always an indicator of wetlands. Resume pines before reaching a second elevated service road at 2.0 miles. The trail is turning westerly here, staying within Collier-Seminole State Park boundaries. A discerning eye will spot faint linear ditches, vestiges of attempts to lower the water table in days gone by, likely to improve pasturage for cattle.

Watch for paint blazes as the trail joins a doubletrack at 2.3 miles, in pine/palm/palmetto. Do not continue on any service road unless you are tracing the paint blazes. At 2.6 miles, the path reenters wetter woods and then meanders to a trail intersection at 2.8 miles. Here, take the spur leading left to the backcountry campsite. Work south, crossing a cypress/maple strand, then reach the simple camp in a palm/live oak hammock at 3.2 miles. Even if you are not overnighting, the spot still makes a decent break spot. Backpackers: remember that you must bring your own water.

Return to the main loop at 3.6 miles. Head left among young slash pines, mixed in with taller evergreens. At 4.1 miles, enter a long trail section that is more cypress than not. You are now in the "wet-footin'-it zone." Depending upon water levels, you will be either sloshing in water or slopping in mud. That is part of the Southwest Florida hiking experience, so embrace it. Unfortunately, some of these cypress areas will also host Brazilian pepper, which, though it creates scenically appealing dark woodlands, also crowds out the native vegetation. Plenty of bromeliads and ferns do remain.

At 5.0 miles, the trail begins its big turn back to the east. Pass a conspicuous wild royal palm on your right; then return to cypress heavy woods, mixed with scattered live oak and laurel oak copses. At 6.4 miles, the path angles northeast from its southeast direction, where it had been roughly following US 41, within earshot, depending on the wind.

From there, the path begins crossing several sloughs, some of them bridged with short boardwalks. Notice the red mangrove lining the creeks. The trail is very mushy between the boardwalks and is bordered with willows in places. At 6.9 miles, the path unexpectedly turns north, aiming for drier ground, found in some ensuing pines. At 7.1 miles, reach a service road. Many hikers turn right here, shortcutting back to the trailhead. But we are going to get the full mileage, so turn right on the service road and then jog left, back on the singletrack hiker path. Explore more woodland mosaic; then complete the loop at 7.3 miles. From here, it is a simple backtrack to finish the trek at 7.4 miles.

Mileages at a Glance

- 0.0 Hiking Adventure Trail trailhead
- 0.1 Right at beginning of loop
- 1.7 Cross service road
- 2.0 Cross a second service road
- 2.8 Spur trail leads left to backcountry campsite
- 3.2 Backcountry campsite
- 3.6 Resume main loop
- 5.0 Curve back east
- 6.4 Cross boardwalks among mangrove-lined streams
- 7.1 Cross service road
- 7.3 Complete the loop
- 7.4 Return to trailhead

37

Royal Palm Nature Trail

Hike Summary: This popular nature trail at Collier-Seminole State Park traverses a tropical hardwood forest as well as an extensive boardwalk. Take a side trip to a wetland marsh, where the freshwater and saltwater Glades intermingle. Start your hike at the attractive boat basin, with its picnic area and boat launch, and then join the shady path, with numerous interpretive stops. The boardwalks provide more open looks at this vegetated wild and wet wonderland. Take your time, looking for wildlife at the wetland marsh overlook before returning to the trailhead.

Lofty palms reach for the sky as you traipse down the boardwalk through Royal Palm Hammock.

Distance: .9-mile loop, including spur to wetland overlook

Hiking Time: 1.0 hours

Difficulty: Easy

Highlights: Tropical hardwood hammock, boardwalk

Cautions: None

Fees/Permits: Entrance fee required

Best Seasons: November through April

Other Trail Users: None. Leashed dogs allowed.

Trail Contacts: Collier-Seminole State Park, 20200 East Tamiami Trail, Naples, FL 34114, (239) 394-3397, www.floridastateparks.org

Finding the Trailhead: From the intersection of US 41 and Collier County Road 951 (Collier Boulevard) on the south end of Naples, drive south on US 41 for 7.6 miles. Enter the state park on your right. Head to the ranger station, and keep forward .1 mile, then turn left at the Barron Collier Memorial, toward the boat ramp/nature trail. Shortly dead-end at the boat-basin parking area. The nature trail will be on your right.

GPS Trailhead Coordinates: N25° 59.308', W81° 35.639'

This is the first trail in Collier-Seminole State Park that visitors encounter, and for many, it is the only one that they end up hiking here. But it is a winner. Be apprised that the path will be busy during winter holidays, when throngs congregate at this visit-worthy state preserve. The trail first traverses a tropical hardwood forest and then heads out on a boardwalk to meet the brackish mangroves, offering incredible biodiversity in one short path. The interpretive information helps visitors comprehend the ecosystem through which they stroll.

Leave the picnic area and boat ramp—a fun place to watch the comings and goings of other visitors and perhaps enjoy a meal of your own—then head north into lush forest. Despite the trail's name, you will not see that many royal palms, but you will walk among gumbo-limbos, live oaks, Jamaica dogwoods, and a junglelike understory of species from Simpson stopper to wild coffee. The forest's thickness recalls movie scenes of explorers hacking through jungles with machetes.

Royal Palm Nature Trail

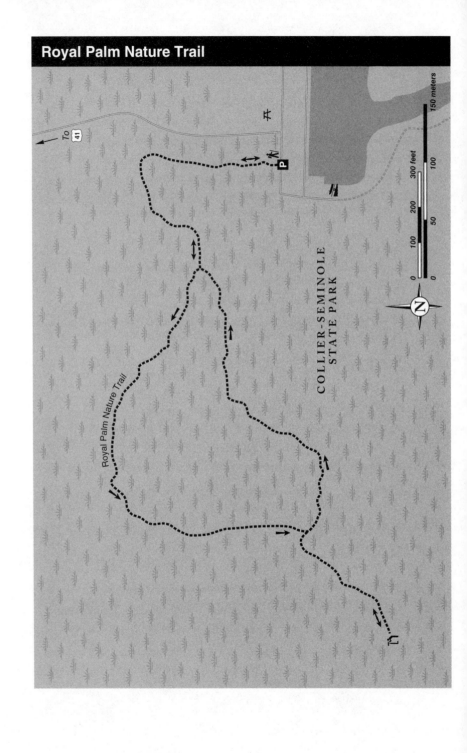

Reach the loop portion of the hike at .2 mile. Stay right with the natural-surface trail, still wandering in dense, dark hammock. Soon reach a long boardwalk traversing a fern field from which rise tall sabal palms. The ferns, palms, and boardwalk produce quite a scene. Thanks to the boardwalk we can walk it dry-footed. At .4 mile, the boardwalk splits. Take the right fork. It leads to an open, wet prairie where grasses and young mangrove trees commingle. Field glasses come in handy for birders. Water depths change seasonally as does the variety of winged creatures.

Backtrack to the main trail, resuming the loop, mostly still on a boardwalk, traversing a salt marsh where red and black mangroves find their places in the spongy terrain. At .7 mile, the path reenters freshwater tropical hardwoods, and the forest canopy closes overhead. All too soon you have completed the loop, leaving a backtrack to the trailhead.

Luckily for us visitors there is plenty more to do here at Collier-Seminole State Park. At the trailhead you can enjoy a picnic, watch the boats come in from the saltwater glades, or even rent a canoe from the park and paddle yourself. Paddlers start out on a canal, but then can ply the northwestern edge of the Everglades. The area is primarily mangrove forest, part of the largest contiguous mangrove forest in the world. These mangrove thickets are encircled by channels that connect the freshwater flowing out of the sawgrass of the Glades and the salty ocean to which the water ultimately flows. Tides move water in and out of these channels where fish thrive and birds make their home overhead. Manatees and alligators also call these waters home.

Collier-Seminole offers an excellent campground amid the tropical landscape. Royal palms sway high overhead. Live oaks and pine form additional tree cover, fashioning the most tropical-looking campground in the state. The campground is busy from after Christmas through April. Snowbirds from the North will stay here during this period for the maximum allotted two weeks before moving on. Get a reservation for weekends during this time. You can usually slip in and get a site during weekdays. After April until the fall cool-down, it's just the mosquitoes, the rangers, and a few hardy souls with a masochistic vein occupying the campground.

The same time frame goes for the backcountry adventurers. Backpackers can take the Hiking Adventure Trail, also detailed in this book, to a campsite in an oak-and-palm hammock. Canoers paddling to the Grocery Place campsite, a smidgen of land enclosed by mangrove, have to bring all their own supplies, but will be rewarded with the solitude of the Everglades.

Finally, be apprised of the many wintertime interpretive ranger programs along with guided walks and paddles. Since the Royal Palm Nature Trail is short, consider timing it with many of the other available activities here.

Mileages at a Glance

0.0 Royal Palm Nature Trail trailhead
0.2 Head right at beginning of loop
0.4 Head right to wetland overlook, backtrack
0.9 Return to trailhead

38

Collier-Seminole Hike/Bike Trail

Hike Summary: Take a walk on the historic side as you trace the old San Marco Road, one of the first auto thoroughfares in Southwest Florida. Follow the old roadbed through the forgotten side of Collier-Seminole State Park, among the pines, palms oaks, and occasional open sawgrass swales. Reach the park boundary and loop back through more forests. Overall, it makes a nice walk. Though the trail is shared with bicyclists, it is favored by more hikers than bikers.

Distance: 3.5-mile loop
Hiking Time: 2.0 hours
Difficulty: Moderate
Highlights: Historic road, varied forests
Cautions: Watch for bicyclists
Fees/Permits: Entrance fee required
Best Seasons: November through April
Other Trail Users: Bicyclists. Leashed dogs allowed.
Trail Contacts: Collier-Seminole State Park, 20200 East Tamiami Trail, Naples, FL 34114, (239) 394-3397, www.floridastateparks.org
Finding the Trailhead: From exit 101 on I-75, take Collier County Road 951 south to US 41. From this intersection, drive south on US 41 for 7.6 miles. Enter the state park on your right. Head to the ranger station and pay your entrance fee. Return to US 41 and head back north for .7 mile, past the intersection with Collier County Road 92. Look left for a grassy parking area on your left just after a small bridge.
GPS Trailhead Coordinates: N25° 59.905', W81° 35.909'

Collier-Seminole Hike/Bike Trail

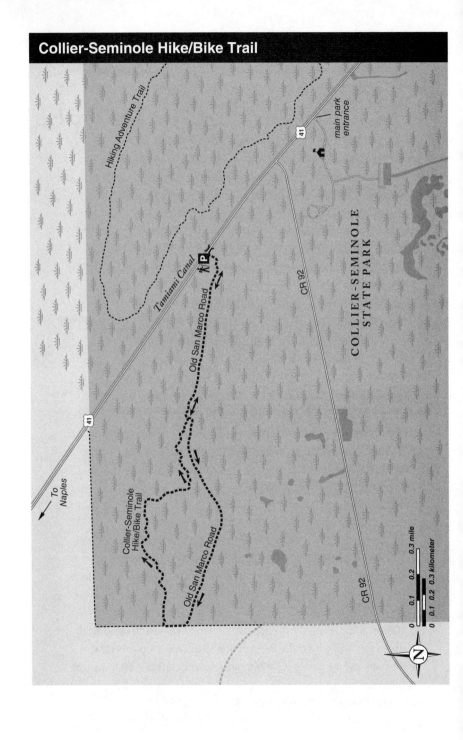

This trail traces the Old San Marco Road.

This path was created in response to requests by bikers for a trail at Collier-Seminole State Park, but hikers have taken a shine to it as well. And getting to follow one of the first traces through this former back of beyond adds a historic element unseen on other area trails. Leave the grassy parking area on US 41 and pass around a gate. Trace a doubletrack sand road south. Stay right with the sand road, passing a second gate. Walk in pine/palm forest; then reach Old San Marco Road. The track turns right, westerly. The Old San Marco Road was constructed a century back, in 1916, when cars first made their way to Southwest Florida. It connected Royal Palm Hammock—the site of today's Collier-Seminole State Park—to Marco Junction at Shell Island. Travelers then reached Marco Island by ferry.

The elevated roadbed leads into more open woodlands dominated by tall slash pine, with brown trunks that reach upward before branching out into boughs of evergreen banked against a blue sky dotted with puffy white clouds. Other areas are more thickly wooded with palm copses and scrub oaks. Small sawgrass clearings occupy other locales. In places, live oaks overhang the trail. A canal, hidden by dense vegetation, parallels the road. The canal provided fill to make the old road and helped drain the track. Imagine the men employed to dredge and grade the road through this wet woodland—the heat, the mosquitoes, and the mud. Then contemplate driving an old Ford Model T and breaking down on a sweltering summer afternoon, only to be stuck far from help, subsequently spending a hot, bug-infested night. It may have happened upon the very stretch that we walk! Southwest Florida's early residents were a tough bunch.

At .6 mile, the trail detours around an environmentally sensitive nesting site. Just before rejoining the Old San Marco Road, you will come to the loop portion of the hike at .7 mile. Continue on the historic road. The path is decently shaded, but sun-exposed open areas may have loose sand, slowing the hiker. Younger live oak stands are making a comeback, and will provide increasing numbers of acorns for wildlife, from squirrels to wild turkeys to black bears.

At 1.1 miles, cross an old canal, usually harboring a gator or two sunning on its banks. Return to pines and palms, where afternoon breezes sway the fronds and needles, whooshing and fluttering, making the sounds of a Florida forest. Pass over another wetland, this one surrounded by bright-green willows. At 1.6 miles, reach the western boundary of Collier-Seminole State Park. Head right here, following a grassy fire road along a fence. At 1.7 miles, leave right from the fire road, now returning easterly. All intersections are clearly marked and signed, leaving you to contemplate the landscape and not navigating.

The loop now meanders through denser woods, going for the most scenic terrain. This part is not elevated like the Old San Marco Road, leaving the footing a little damper, but under normal conditions, winter hikers should still make the entire trek dry-footed. The more lush forest affords enhanced shade. At 2.8 miles, complete the circuit. From here, backtrack, retracing the Old San Marco Road before reaching the trailhead and US 41 at 3.5 miles.

Mileages at a Glance

- 0.0 Collier-Seminole Hike/Bike Trail trailhead on US 41
- 0.1 Join Old San Marco Road
- 0.7 Begin loop portion of hike
- 1.6 Right at state park boundary
- 1.7 Turn east back toward trailhead
- 2.8 Complete the loop, backtrack
- 3.5 Return to trailhead

39

Marsh Trail

Hike Summary: This trail at Ten Thousand Islands National Wildlife Refuge is a birders' paradise. An elevated track leads you into the estuarine waters of the refuge as it changes from freshwater to salt water. The path starts out paved and leads to a wildlife observation tower, delivering a commanding view of the land and waterscape, ideal for seeing birdlife below. The rest of the trail is crushed gravel and travels past more ponds dotted with mangrove islands.

Bird watchers flock to this tower at Ten Thousand Islands National Wildlife Refuge.

Distance: 2.4-mile there-and-back

Hiking Time: 2.0 hours

Difficulty: Easy

Highlights: Wildlife viewing tower, birds

Cautions: Trailside alligators

Fees/Permits: No fees or permits required

Best Seasons: Year-round

Other Trail Users: None. No dogs allowed.

Trail Contacts: Ten Thousand Islands National Wildlife Refuge, 3860 Tollgate Blvd., Suite 300, Naples, FL 34114, (239) 353-8442, www.fws. gov/floridapanther/TenThousandIslands/

Finding the Trailhead: From the intersection of US 41 and Collier County Road 951(Collier Boulevard) on the south end of Naples, drive south on US 41 for 11 miles. Look for the open parking area on your right.

GPS Trailhead Coordinates: N25° 58.450', W81° 33.244'

Birders and other wildlife enthusiasts will be well rewarded on this trail. In the wintertime it is crowded with another kind of wildlife known as snowbirds, the Yankees who come down here from the colder states, well beyond Florida's border. Furthermore, very few visitors hike it at a brisk pace. Rather they amble the track, stopping to observe an alligator lazing in the sun, a flock of ibis flying overhead, or, if they're lucky, roseate spoonbills feeding in the shallows. So come and enjoy the Marsh Trail and plan to take your time. The entire route is open to the sun overhead, so have a hat, sunscreen, and water with you during your hike.

The trail leaves the open parking area, which doubles as a canoe-trail launch, and crosses a wetland by a bridge to join a gravel asphalt trail heading south. The marsh around the trailhead is freshwater. Note the cattails and sawgrass. The path is bordered by willows, myrtle, and the occasional gumbo-limbo or small live oak tree. Ferns and grasses grow thick below the foliage. A canal runs along the trail at first. The waterway is where

Marsh Trail

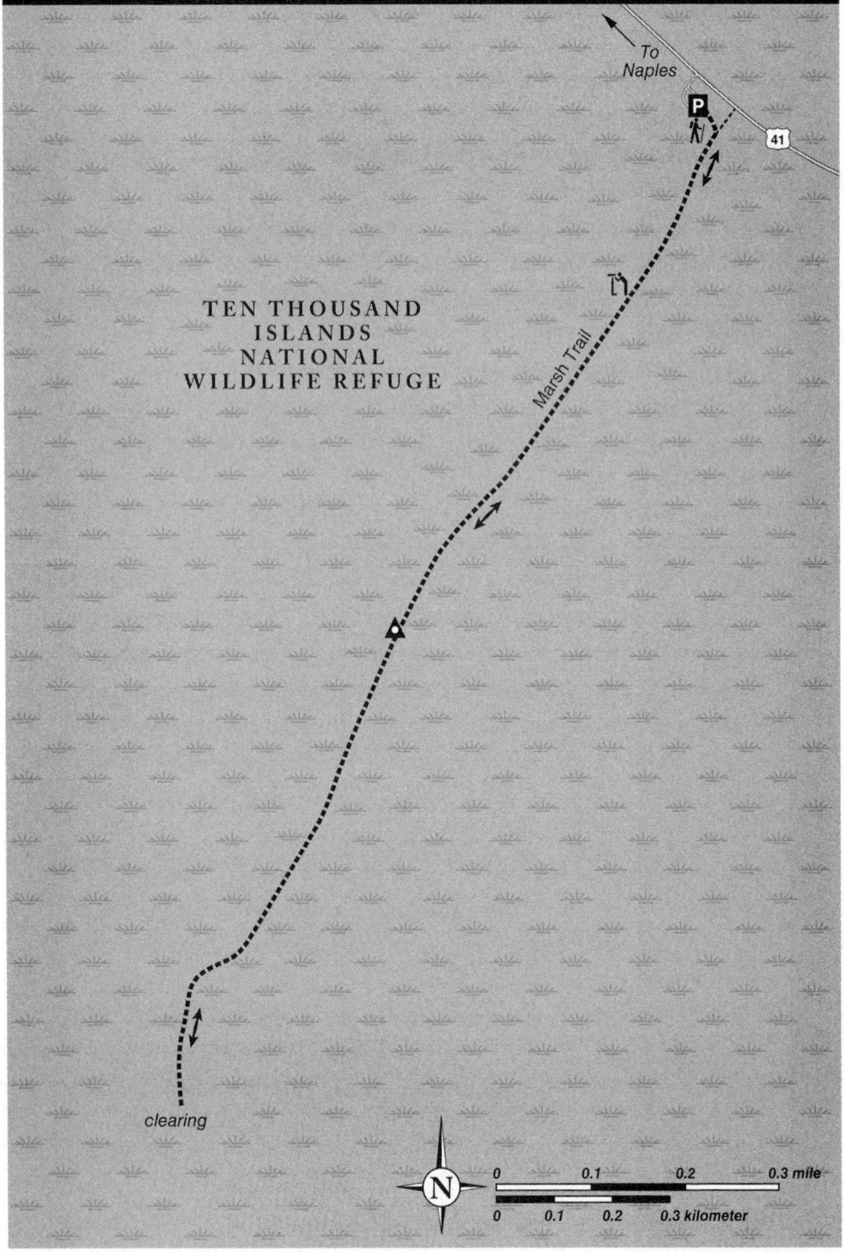
To
Naples
P
41
TEN THOUSAND
ISLANDS
NATIONAL
WILDLIFE REFUGE
Marsh Trail
clearing
N
0
0.1
0.2
0.3 mile
0
0.1
0.2
0.3 kilometer

Birds of different feathers flock together at this refuge.

swamp neophytes stand enthralled at the site of reptiles, but for Florida residents, seeing an alligator is nothing new.

The canal soon gives way to scattered ponds, open wetlands, and shallows dotted with mangrove islets. Birders toting binoculars and camera will be snapping photos and adding to their life list of birds observed. The asphalt track ends at the observation tower. A ramp allows all access to the tower's lower tier. Steps lead to an upper observation area, perched more than 30 feet above the ground. Here, field glasses are available for anyone to observe the scene below. You will see an interface of land and water, and estuarine habitats where salt and freshwater commingle, a rich environment for the entire food chain.

Ten Thousand Islands National Wildlife Refuge, established in 1996, is more water than land. Its upper reaches receive freshwater flow from Fakahatchee and Picayune Strands, then flow to the Gulf, where a plethora of mangrove isles form an aquatic jigsaw puzzle and give the refuge its name. An estimated 10 percent of Florida's manatees use the refuge. The waters and islands of the refuge also provide vital habitat and nesting zones for loggerhead turtles. Just a few minutes on this trail will bear out the refuge's importance for avian wildlife. These islands were once home to Southwest Florida's Calusa Indians, who ruled a pre-Columbian empire from present-day Tampa down to the Keys.

Continue down a crushed gravel path. Mangrove now lines much of the trail, though ample open areas allow panoramas into the scattered ponds and marsh. At .6 mile, the berm widens and a contemplation bench overlooks a shallow where mangrove trees are seemingly placed at random. From this vantage it is easy to see how the Ten Thousand Islands got its name. Imagine an aerial view or, better yet, use the Internet to get an aerial view of the Ten Thousand Islands, and you will see how it got its second name—the Mangrove Maze.

Pass a culvert connecting the wetlands to your right and left. This is another alligator hangout. You will also see flattened areas where the ancient creatures lie along the shore, sunning for warmth. The cold-blooded beasts dislike chilly weather as much as the snowbirds flocking to Southwest Florida. The trail continues its southerly Gulf-bound direction before reaching a wide clearing at 1.2 miles. Here, you will see a weather observation station in the clearing's center. To your left is a mangrove-lined waterway. The path ends at a contemplation bench dead ahead, which overlooks a seasonal wetland. On your backtrack, you will undoubtedly see more wildlife, namely birds such as egrets.

Mileages at a Glance

0.0 Marsh Trail trailhead
0.2 Come to the observation tower
0.6 Reach a wide spot in the trail with contemplation bench
1.2 End an open area with weather station
2.4 Return to trailhead

40

Big Cypress Bend Boardwalk

Hike Summary: This short trek starts at a Miccosukee Indian village on the edge of Fakahatchee Strand Preserve State Park. It follows an old tram road and then enters a junglelike hardwood hammock on a winding boardwalk. Walk beneath huge cypresses

The board-walk takes you right by gigantic cypress trees such as this one.

and strangler figs in a riot of vegetational variety. A bald-eagle nest highlights the wildlife viewing opportunities.

Distance: 1.2-mile there-and-back
Hiking Time: 1.0 hours
Difficulty: Easy
Highlights: Plant biodiversity, hardwood hammock, eagle's nest
Cautions: Crowded path
Fees/Permits: No fees or permits required
Best Seasons: November through April
Other Trail Users: None. No dogs allowed.
Trail contacts: Fakahatchee Strand Preserve State Park, 137 Coastline Drive, Copeland, FL 34137, (239) 695-4593, www.floridastateparks.org
Finding the Trailhead: From the intersection of US 41 and Collier County Road 951 (Collier Boulevard) on the south end of Naples, drive south on US 41 for 17 miles. Look for the brown sign for the boardwalk. You will also see a sign that reads "Indian Village" just at the parking area, on your left.
GPS Trailhead Coordinates: N25° 56.518', W81° 28.166'

This hike can be busy with accidental tourists. Drivers on US 41 see the sign for Big Cypress Bend Boardwalk and then suddenly pull in, also attracted by the Indian village adjacent to the trailhead. No matter what brought them there, hikers will enjoy this trek into a thick swamp forest. This tropical woodland is a natural highlight of Fakahatchee Strand Preserve State Park, a 5 × 20–mile swath of wildness where panthers and black bears roam and orchids thrive undisturbed. This nature experience is a microcosm of the Fakahatchee, a place where Florida's state butterfly, the zebra longwing, flutters to your delight.

Avoid this trail on winter holiday weekends—the crowds can get thick. Leave the park area on US 41, crossing the roadside canal. Enter the trail on the south side of the fenced Indian Village; then pass a kiosk detailing Fakahatchee Strand Preserve State Park as well as a donation box. Another canal lies off to your right as you walk away from the road. Birds and alligators

Big Cypress Bend Boardwalk

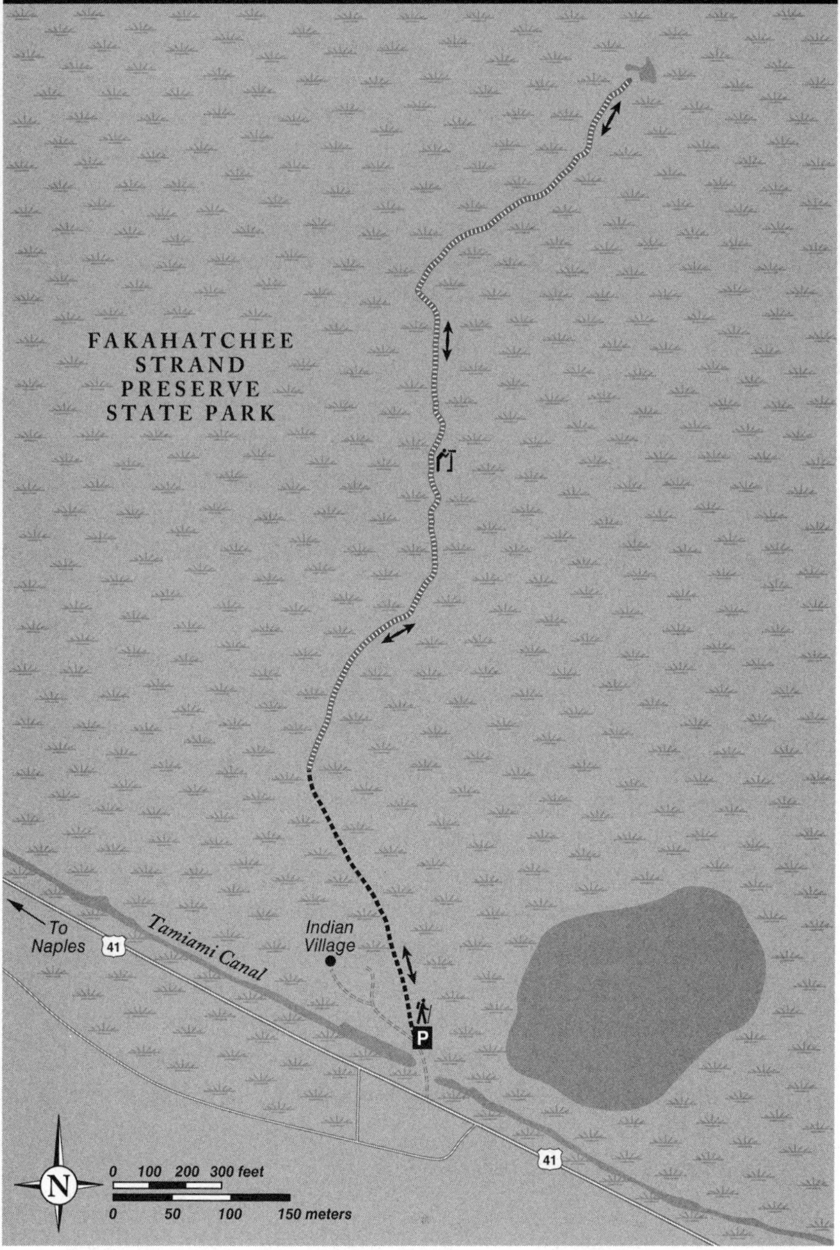

FAKAHATCHEE
STRAND
PRESERVE
STATE PARK

To
Naples 41

Tamiami Canal

Indian
Village

P

41

N

0   100 200 300 feet

0   50   100   150 meters

Royal palm in its native habitat.

draw tourists to the water. Live oaks, laurel oaks, cypresses, red maples, and palms shade the track. Interpretive signage enhances your experience. So many plants to learn about! At .2 mile, the wide, roadlike path reaches the narrower, elevated wooden boardwalk. Leave the land and canal behind, immersing in a tropical hardwood forest—lush, cool, and full of life in any season, a place echoing in birdsong where the ground is covered in green ferns and regal royal palms and sturdy cypress rise in glory. Binocular-laden hikers can be found on this trail, too.

Your footfalls make light thuds as you step forth over the winding walkway, stopping here to read an interpretive sign, stopping there to look up close at a strangler fig enveloping a cypress, or to watch a squirrel hop from tree to tree. Nowadays we see royal palms everywhere, planted along roads in cities and adorning suburban shopping centers, but they were once rare. Here, you can see wild royal palms in various stages of growth, their concrete-like trunks ever-thickening.

Down the way, the boardwalk widens. Here, the deck is built around a pair of massive bald-cypress trees. These two voluminous giants rise high into the hardwood hammock canopy, availing an up-close opportunity to truly appreciate their size and age. Such behemoths lured loggers to South Florida's swamp woods. Much of the Fakahatchee was cut down. Miles of logging tram roads were left after the axes ceased chopping, but the Fakahatchee has recovered well. Still other areas, such as along this walk, were never harvested. The density of this forest is amazing, where hardly a space is left unclaimed, from the alligator flag rising from the wetter places to wild coffee, which isn't really coffee, sporting its electric-green leaves.

Another highlight of the hike is an eagle's nest, visible from the boardwalk. The park has even built a tripod stand into the boardwalk for the photographers, who ply this wooden walkway in great numbers. There may be a photographer-jam on nice weekends at this point. A pair of bald eagles has nested here since 1985, and you can see the nest set high in a tree. Binoculars aid in discerning detail. Eagle nests can be as large as 20 feet wide and 9 feet deep!

Somewhere along the way, use one of the contemplation benches to stop, relax, and let the wilderness come to you. Sometimes, when we are still, we will detect the movement of wildlife more easily. Such a bench is located at trail's end, overlooking a shallow swamp pond that is often green with duck moss, where herons and other birds stalk the shallows for minnows and other goodies to eat. It is all part of the experience on the Big Cypress Bend Boardwalk.

Mileages at a Glance

0.0 Big Cypress Bend Boardwalk trailhead
0.2 Join the boardwalk
0.6 End of boardwalk at a swamp pond, backtrack
1.2 Return to trailhead

JOHNNY MOLLOY is a writer and adventurer based in Johnson City, Tennessee, who spends his winters in Florida.

The results of his efforts are more than fifty books and guides. His writings include guidebooks for hiking, camping, and paddling, as well as comprehensive guidebooks about specific areas. He also writes true outdoor adventure books set throughout the eastern United States.

Besides his books, Molloy writes for magazines and websites and is a columnist and feature writer for his local newspaper, the *Johnson City Press*. He continues to travel and engage in a variety of outdoor pursuits. For the latest on Johnny, please visit www.johnnymolloy.com.

Other Books by Johnny Molloy

50 Hikes in the North Georgia Mountains
50 Hikes in the Ozarks
50 Hikes in South Carolina
60 Hikes within 60 Miles: San Antonio & Austin (with Tom Taylor)
60 Hikes within 60 Miles: Nashville
A Canoeing & Kayaking Guide to the Streams of Florida (with Elizabeth Carter)
A Canoeing & Kayaking Guide to the Streams of Kentucky (with Bob Sehlinger)
Backcountry Fishing: A Guide for Hikers, Paddlers, and Backpackers
Beach and Coastal Camping in Florida
Beach and Coastal Camping in the Southeast
The Best in Tent Camping: The Carolinas
The Best in Tent Camping: Colorado (with Kim Lipker)
The Best in Tent Camping: Florida
The Best in Tent Camping: Georgia
The Best in Tent Camping: Kentucky
The Best in Tent Camping: Southern Appalachian and Smoky Mountains
The Best in Tent Camping: Tennessee
The Best in Tent Camping: West Virginia
The Best in Tent Camping: Wisconsin (with Kevin Revolinski)
Day & Overnight Hikes along Kentucky's Sheltowee Trace
Day & Overnight Hikes, Great Smoky Mountains National Park
Day & Overnight Hikes, Shenandoah National Park
Day & Overnight Hikes, West Virginia's Monongahela National Forest
From the Swamp to the Keys: A Paddle through Florida History
Hiking the Florida Trail: 1,100 Miles, 78 Days, Two Pairs of Boots, and One Heck of an Adventure
Hiking Mississippi
Mount Rogers National Recreation Area Guidebook
The Hiking Trails of Florida's National Forests, Parks, and Preserves (with Sandra Friend)
Land Between The Lakes Outdoor Recreation Handbook
Long Trails of the Southeast
Paddling Tennessee
Paddling Georgia
Trial By Trail: Backpacking in the Smoky Mountains